It is better to wait long than to marry wrong. Invest in the knowledge-ware to enjoy a marriage free of despair.

AFTER YOU SAY "I DO"

21 CONSIDERATIONS FOR CONSTRUCTING A THRIVING MARRIAGE

The Matched and Attached Book Series

Nicholas Robertson & Danielle Brown-Robertson

AFTER YOU SAY I DO:21 CONSIDERATIONS FOR CONSTRUCTING A THRIVING MARRIAGE

Published by:

ISBN: 978-1-990266-54-6

Scripture references are taken from the Message Version of the Bible.

All Emphasis in scripture quotations were added by the author.

Contact Us at couples.corner@positivevibrationglobal.com

Cover design by: Iconic Presence

JOIN OUR COMMUNITY

You may subscribe to our mailing list to be among the first group to receive information about our new releases, Matched and Attached seminars, courses and 21 Shades Beta club activities. Follow the links below to our website, YouTube channel and other social media pages.

- https://www.positivevibrationglobal.com/contact
- https://www.youtube.com/c/THEROBDONS
- https://www.facebook.com/therobdons
- https://www.instagram.com/mrs_robdon/
- https://www.instagram.com/pillowtalkglobal/
- https://www.facebook.com/pillowtalkglobal

Email us: info@positivebrationglobal.com

Table of Contents

FOREWORD

"After You Say I Do: 21 Considerations for Constructing a Thriving Marriage," invites you to embark on a transformative journey through this heartfelt guidebook meticulously crafted to fortify the foundation of love and commitment. As you delve into the pages, you'll discover essential insights, actionable advice, and thought-provoking reflections that illuminate the path toward a resilient and joy-filled union. From enduring challenges to fostering emotional intimacy, this book serves as a comprehensive roadmap for couples, offering practical guidance on communication, trust, and mutual understanding. Whether you're at the beginning of your marital journey or seeking to enrich an existing partnership, unlock the keys to a fulfilling and enduring marriage. Join the exploration of endurance, forgiveness, empathy, and more, as you navigate the convolutions of a lifelong commitment. This guide is not just a collection of principles; it's a companion on your journey, providing the tools to navigate common challenges and build a lasting bond. As you turn the pages, embrace the wisdom within and empower your marriage with the insights needed to construct a thriving, lifelong connection.

Deacon Norman Brown & Pastor Florence Hylton-Brown
Authors' Parents, Ministers, and Counsellors

STATEMENT OF VALIDATION

In '**After You Say I Do: 21 Considerations for Constructing a Thriving Marriage**,' The Robdons eloquently weaves together profound insights and practical advice, creating a guide that transcends the clichés of marital bliss. This book is a beacon for couples seeking not just longevity but genuine fulfilment in their journey together. With a thoughtful exploration of 21 crucial considerations, The Robdons imparts wisdom that is both relatable and transformative. A must-read for anyone committed to building a resilient and joyous marriage.

Mr & Mrs Black
Marriage Officer and Counsellor

STATEMENT OF VALIDATION

Captivating and insightful, **'After You Say I Do: 21 Considerations for Constructing a Thriving Marriage'** is a must-read guide for anyone embarking on the journey of matrimony. With wisdom and practicality, The Robdons offers a roadmap to navigate the complexities of marriage, providing invaluable insights that go beyond the wedding day. This book is a beacon of hope for couples, fostering a foundation for a resilient and flourishing partnership. A compelling read that resonates long after the final page.

Rev & Mrs Carter
Minister of Religion, Marriage Therapist & Podcast Host

PRODUCT USER GUIDE

Meter, Cues & Gauges

Before reading each principle, rate your knowledge of the area using the gauge.

Low- I have little knowledge about this area.

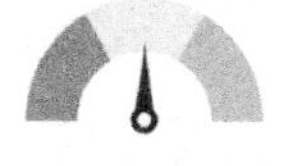

Moderate- I have some knowledge about this area but need to know more.

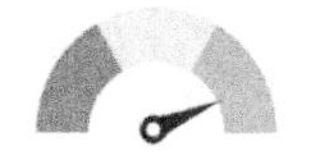

High - I know a lot about this area.

Read each principle and carefully analyse your partner and relationship. Circle the flag light to determine how well you and spouse are excelling at each principle shared in this book.

I do not believe my partner/myself possess these qualities and thus believe if I proceed into marriage the union will not thrive.

I do not believe my partner/myself possess these qualities to an extent but needs some work before proceeding into marriage. If

I do believe that my partner/myself possesses these qualities and thus believe we can proceed into marriage. If we do the union is

PRODUCT GUARANTEE

Dear couples,

We guarantee that as you read this book, you will have a greater understanding of the principles that, when observed, lead to thriving marriages. It includes our personal stories, knowledge through experiences, and valuable information acquired through training. Now, having said I do, this book is amongst the best resources. Invest in your marriage by reading and applying today.

Marriage is a daily discipline; you must choose to share your heart in every situation. Commit to constantly learning and exploring new ventures together to guarantee a successful marriage. Marriage is not an upgrade to a better life; it is an opportunity to have another fulfilling experience. Do not live thinking you are inadequate or incomplete. Your marriage is what you make it. Become a worthwhile productive individual working assiduously to create a thriving union.

Feel free to ask about our 21 Shades Beta Club and delve into the wealth we share as you craft a beautiful narrative for intimacy in your marriage. Check out our other resources on empowering singles and couples to triumph at marriage.

Signed,

THE ROBDONS, Your Optimists.

CAUTION!!

This resource is not your typical 'over' religious book on marriage. It contains a good mix between theology, psychology, and other related fields. The lessons are informative, comprehensive, awe-inspiring, and actionable. Have an open mind as you engage with **"After You Say I Do: 21 Considerations for Constructing a Thriving Marriage."**

THE MUST & MUST NOT

REGULATORY COMPLIANCE FOR MARRIAGE CONSTRUCTION

THE MUSTS

- Read through all the principles in this book.
- Reflect on content presented in this book.
- Discuss the questions written in each principle and any other that may arise.
- Be honest when evaluating and completing the flag light.

THE MUSTS NOTS

- Ignore any answer to questions that may conflicting with yours.
- Refuse to alter behaviour improve your relationship.
- Avoid communication, neglect emotional needs, and harbour resentment.
- Take each other for granted or allow external stressors to dominate your marriage.
- Neglect self-care and personal honesty.

PROGRESS-METER

Welcome to your After You Say I do journey! By the end of reading this book, you will be equipped to use your ***progress-meter*** to determine how well the marriage is thriving. See PROGRESS-METER DECISION REPORT.

How would you describe your knowledge about creating a thriving marriage? Shade your response on the progress-meter below. Be sure to give details on the lines explaining the reason for your answer. Finally set specific goals you anticipate achieving at the end of this journey.

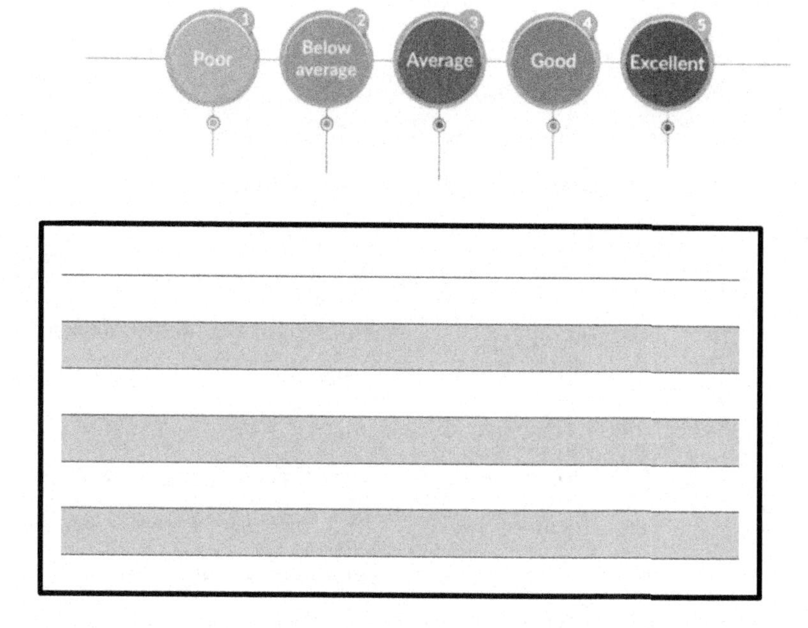

THE LAUNCH

Welcome to **After You Say I Do: 21 Considerations for Constructing a Thriving Marriage**. In this book, we delve into the intricate tapestry of a successful and fulfilling partnership. Marriage, an exquisite journey of companionship, demands careful cultivation and profound understanding. Within these pages, we explore the essential considerations, timeless principles, and practical insights that fortify the bonds of love and create a resilient foundation for a thriving and enduring relationship. Join me as we embark on a journey to uncover the keys to a fulfilling and lasting marriage."

Marriage is a beautiful institution, and anyone who have undertaken the journey should be open to some of the key considerations that will be important to the success.

Every piece of equipment comes with a manual that tells the user how to operate it according to the manufacturer's guidelines for maximum efficiency. No matter how experienced the user is, the instructions are usually clear enough that even a novice can fulfil the expectations with a significant level of mastery. Like all equipment, marriage requires support, understanding, and clarity. The idea of marriage is of God; therefore, the primary manual for ensuring a thriving marriage is the Bible. **After you say I Do: 21 Considerations for Constructing a Thriving Marriage,** however, is a tool intended to simplify and bring to light the principles guaranteeing a successful marriage, drawing from the author's own experiences alongside their psychological and educational expertise to bolster your awareness.

The writers intend to:

- help couples build a more fulfilling life together.

Explore this resource with an open mind, allowing yourself to be open to learning. Work together with your spouse to embrace the principles that ensure a successful and thriving union. Craft your personalised formula for a thriving relationship.

EXPRESSION OF GRATITUDE

"It is somewhat flawed to attain great successes and disacknowledge the contribution of those who played an integral role on the journey, directly or indirectly. It takes the prudent who understands the importance and effect of collaboration to offer recognition with appreciation,"- **Unknown.**

We are deeply honoured to acknowledge the individuals whose contributions have been integral to the success of this resource. As believers in a higher power, we express immense gratitude to God for the wisdom that guided the creation of every page within this content. To our close friends who lent us their ears and offered sincere feedback, your invaluable insights played a pivotal role in this unforgettable journey, and for that, we are eternally thankful.

A heartfelt appreciation goes out to Oneil Brown from iconence.com, our creative graphics partner, whose artistic touch elevated the presence of **"After You say I do: 21 Considerations for Constructing a Thriving Marriage."** Your dedication to delivering top-notch quality products and services is commendable.

Gratitude extends to The Blacks and The Carters for investing their time in reading and endorsing this engaging and thought-provoking relationship tool. To The Browns, your eloquent foreword offers an excellent overview of the enclosed message. Your ongoing support and guidance mean the world to us.

Lastly, we extend our thanks to every individual committed to reading this book. We eagerly anticipate your insightful feedback and, more importantly, your stories of a transformative journey in marriage. We gratefully acknowledge your unwavering contributions and hope that you'll share this content, as together, we aim to cultivate an environment capable of positively impacting the world, starting with strong and thriving marriages.

MARRIAGE, ENDURANCE AND PERSEVERANCE

Enduring Love: The Power of Perseverance in Overcoming Challenges in Marriage.

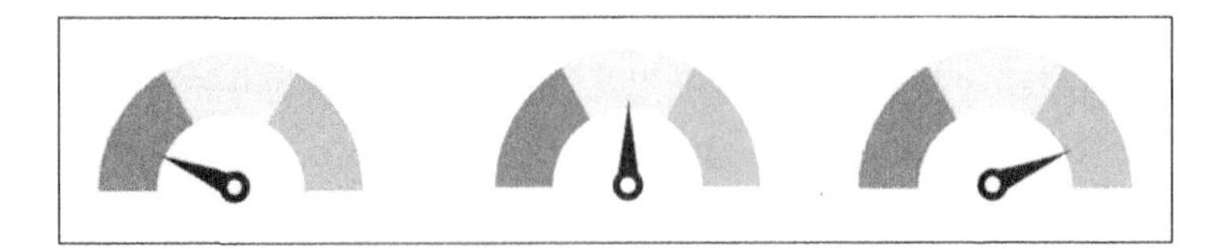

"Love doesn't sit there like a stone, it has to be made, like bread; remade every day, made new." — Unknown

During my early years, my mentor shared a story with me about a railway engine.

A little railroad engine was employed about a station yard for such work as it was built for, pulling a few cars on and off the switches. One morning it was waiting for the next call when a long train of freight cars asked a large engine in the roundhouse to take it over the hill. "I can't; that is too much of a pull for me," said the great engine built for hard work.

Then the train asked another engine, and another, only to hear excuses and be refused. In desperation, the train asked the little switch engine to draw it up the grade and down on the other side. "I think I can", puffed the little locomotive, and put itself in front of the great heavy train. As it went on the little engine kept bravely puffing faster and faster, "I think I can, I think I can, I think I can."

As it neared the top of the grade, which had so discouraged the larger engines, it went more slowly. However, it kept saying, "I—think—I—can, I—think—I—can." It reached the top by drawing on bravery and then went on down the grade, congratulating itself by saying, "I thought I could, I thought I could."

Like the large railroad engine, many people cower in fear of the demands and expectations that accompany marriage, constantly feeling unprepared or unable to satisfy each other's needs.

What do people fear most about marriage?

Data collected from varying couples over the years yielded the extent of people's fear relating to marriage:

- fear of getting hurt.
- fear of commitment.
- fear inadequacy.
- fear of frequent arguments.
- fear of change.
- fear of missing out on youthful ambitions.
- fear of being judged.
- fear of deception.
- fear of submission.
- fear of unhappiness.
- fear of falling out of love.

Each fear is represented by the extensive load stocked onto the train in the story, who requested help to get over the hill. Even the most prominent and capable railroad engines were unwilling to commit to the task of getting a loaded train over the hill. Like the more capable trains, some people find the thought of marriage extremely overwhelming; thus, many choose to remain unmarried. Interestingly, people do not remain single; they remain unmarried. They are opposed to the relationship and its demands; they are concerned about the moral, ethical, and legal concerns relating to marriage. Somehow, the absence of commitment reduces the effect, lessens the burdens, and creates a safe space to function free of moral obligations.

Within every individual is a burning passion to succeed at anything they commit to. However, people would rather not start a challenge than fail at trying. The small railroad engine, however, teaches an essential lesson: Begin the challenge of marriage knowing you can. As you persist daily, remind yourself that you can love, forgive, serve, submit to, empower, and care for your spouse." A great marriage isn't something that just happens; it's something that must be created." – Fawn Weaver

Consequently, marriage must begin with the will to take small, tiny, continuous, and intentional steps to succeed.

Please note that it is not the size of the dog but the bite of the dog that matters. Similarly, commitment to marriage should not be measured by your socioeconomic status but by your mental acuity. Readiness begins with your mind: Are you willing to stick to it until you succeed?

> "For better, for worse, for richer, for poorer, in sickness and in health, to love and to cherish, till death we do part, according to God's holy law, and this is my solemn vow."
>
> - extract from the marriage vow.

No matter what happens, we have decided to love, commit to, and serve each other in our marriages. Just like the small railroad engine, do not give up under pressure or in the presence of adversity. Surely, if you stick to it, you will encounter the desired outcome. The pursuit to a successful marriage must begin with the right attitude, knowing that you can be faithful, loving, caring, honest, supportive, communicate effectively, act decisively, trust and serve. "A perfect marriage is just two imperfect people who refuse to give up on each other." – Unknown

People start the journey through marriage to succeed, not to fail. Working on the desired marriage is the most intense project you and your spouse will ever have to complete. You can't take breaks, you can't give up, and even with the help of counsellors you and your spouse must complete the work of marriage. You must forgive, love, cherish, and serve; marriage requires your actions. The constant support, understanding, forgiveness, and service to each other can feel like a tumultuous task, but it will be worth it in the end. Good testimonies are the result of risk-taking, believing in your abilities, and your undeniable trust in God. "A great marriage is not when the 'perfect couple' comes together. It is when an imperfect couple learns to enjoy their differences." – Dave Meurer

With a mind willing to try and the will to fulfil the promise made to each other, you will exceed expectations, surpass the bumps, learn new lessons, and succeed in marriage.

Danielle and I had to quickly unlearn most societal norms from the onset of our union because we understood that the scriptures and not society define the work of marriage. During our period of courtship, I recall having an intense discussion about marriage, and we needed to make it work. This, of course, was on the heels of one of our extensive counselling sessions. As we reflected on the high demands accompanying our desire to marry, we plunged into a trance more like a wonderland scene from our favourite Hallmark movie. "Hun, do you think we have the right attitude, wisdom, knowledge, understanding, and support to succeed in marriage?" Notice our questions were properly formatted to suit our religious conviction but lacked any concern for realism. Danielle responded, "No, we don't, but we can commit to try." At the time, we were first-year tertiary education students; what could we really know about marriage? This was by far the most reflective period of the premarital marathon. "Whatever you vividly imagine, ardently desire, sincerely believe, and enthusiastically act upon... must inevitably come to pass!" — Paul J. Meyer

Danielle's assertive response comforted me and inspired me to know I was worthy, capable, and adequate. No one will ever be completely ready for marriage, but a willingness to try and stick to it will bring you smiles, joy, and peace in the future. Success is not given; it is earned.

That evening after we separated, I reflected on my own struggles and the thought of readiness for marriage. Even up to the day of the proposal, I wondered if I was ready. Undoubtedly, I loved Danielle and knew I wanted to be her "Knight and Shining star," but what if I failed? You can't possibly know everything that will happen in a marriage, but you can make a commitment to persist regardless of the challenges experienced. This must be the couple's mutual commitment; no matter what, "I will not give up on you". Fear erects roadblocks that are visible only to you. Some challenges are merely a figment of your imagination. Overcome your fear of commitment, knowing God has equipped you to succeed.

"For God has not given us a spirit of fear and timidity, but of power, love, and self-discipline." — 2 Timothy 1:7 (NLT)

During that week, I struggled with the idea of marriage, not because I didn't love her but because I didn't want to fail in my quest to make her happy. You couldn't blame me; after all, so many seemingly committed people failed miserably at marriage. Just that week, Joe, an ardent Christian businessman and the son of Bishop James, divorced his wife. They were more financially stable, spiritually aligned, and emotionally intelligent, yet they, like the larger engine in the story, gave up on trying to make the marriage work. They had no interest in continuing their marriage despite frequent prayers and spiritual advice offered to them by friends and family. How can the son of the bishop be so ready to divorce his wife of three years? I thought to myself, marriage must really be difficult.

Marriage is indeed hard work, but it will be worth every minute dedicated to practising the right qualities to ensure its success. "Productivity is never an accident. It is always the result of a commitment to excellence, intelligent planning, and focused effort." — Paul J. Meyer

Not only is marriage beautiful when we excel at it, but it gives a rewarding feeling to know that you have partnered with, shared your dream and vision with, spent quality time with, and relied on in both the good and bad times, creating valuable and lasting memories with your spouse. Dragging the train over the top was not going to be easy, but the little engine was willing to try. Successful marriages emerge from a simple will to keep trying. Repeating this desire continuously will eventually mature into meaningful life lessons, moments of laughter, and never-ending joy. Like the little engine, a time will come when you will be happy you chose to undertake the challenge of remaining together.

There is joy in sticking together in marriage; make every effort to love and serve each other through the good and bad times. Marriage does not fail because of a curse instilled but because people make the same poor choices. Even if you are the president of the free world, the success of marriage depends on the will to commit. We will all experience challenging times in our union, but we will succeed if we stick to our commitment.

Any marriage's success requires the ongoing commitment of each member. The failure of other marriages does not indicate your marriage will automatically fail. It is practising the same bad habits that will eventually produce the same unfavourable results. We must, therefore, endeavour to love, serve, and care for each other if we are to produce favourable results in marriage. Let us stick to it and continue in love.

Husbands, love your wives [with an affectionate, sympathetic, selfless love that always seeks the best for them] and do not be embittered or resentful toward them [because of the responsibilities of marriage] — Colossians 3:19.

It is inexcusable to deny our wives the love, care, and respect. We are husbands and not tyrants. We commit to these elementary values whether we think they deserve it or not.

Our wives do not need to qualify for our love and forgiveness; we love them regardless.

Dear husbands,

Let us stick to treating our wives with affection and not as objects of satisfaction.

Love is a deliberate attitude that concerns itself with the well-being of the one loved. In its purest sense love must be:

- unchangeable.
- self-giving, that is, given without demanding or expecting repayment.
- unmatched, a love so great that it can be given to the unlovable or unappealing.
- love that loves even when it is rejected. it is love that gives and loves because it wants to; it does not demand or expect repayment from the love given. it gives because it loves, it does not love to receive.

Dear wives,

Commit to serve the interest of their spouse even if it is unpopular. Be subject to your own husbands, as [a service] to the Lord. For the husband is head of the wife, as Christ is head of the church, Himself being the Saviour of the body. But as the church is subject to Christ, so also wives should be subject to their husbands in everything [respecting both their position as protector and their responsibility to God as head of the house].

Dear couple,

The success of the marriage is founded on the selfless commitment of the participants to keep trying. It is true that we will not always get it right, but we must never desist from trying. We are now years into our marriage. Danielle and I continue to commit to not giving up on each other and our commitment to each other. "A husband and wife may disagree on many things, but they must absolutely agree on this: to never, ever give up." —Unknown

Reflect Now That You Have Proceeded...

Circle the flag light that best describes your assessment of yourself/ partner based on the topic: **Marriage and Perseverance.**

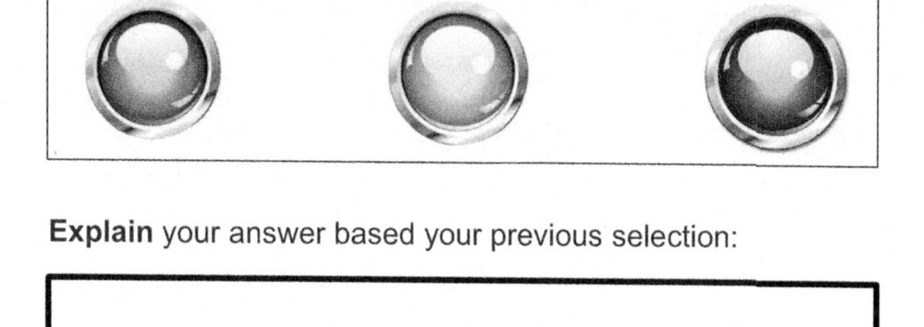

Explain your answer based your previous selection:

Know-Metre: Now appraise your knowledge of this topic after reading by circling the gauge.

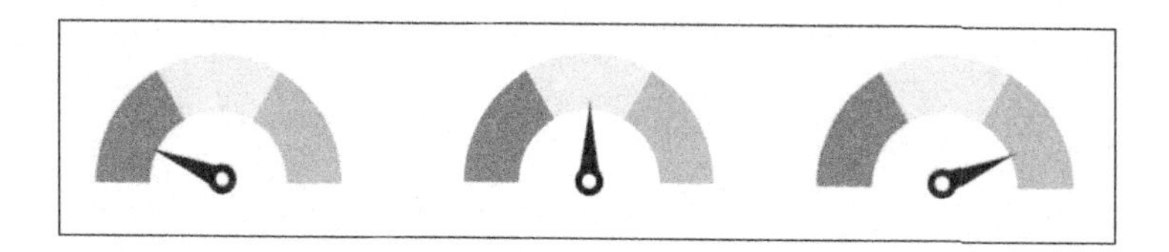

MARRIAGE AND PROBLEM SOLVING

Building a Strong Foundation: Effective Problem-Solving Strategies for Healthy and Resilient Marriage.

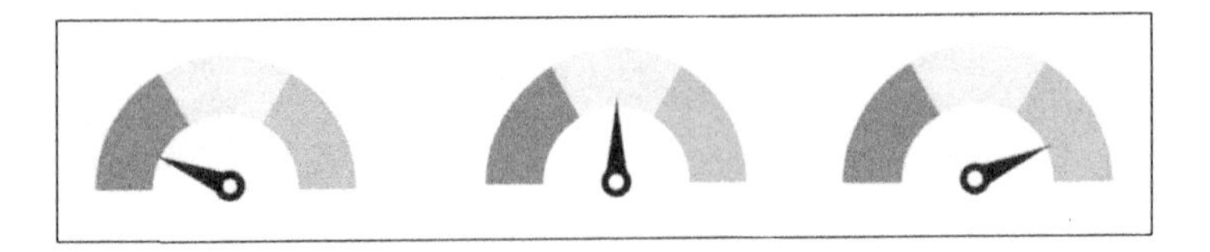

"You come to love not by finding the right person, but by seeing an imperfect person perfectly." — Sam Keen

We got married as two amateurs, ages 21 and 25, fresh out of college with no prior serious experience in intimate relationships. Yes, we had just participated in an extraordinarily detailed and practical premarital counselling program, but still, marriage brought some unanticipated challenges. The loud shouts and screams at your ceremony do not accurately represent your life together after the wedding. We had several family members and friends cheering us on when we disclosed our intent to get married, but after our wedding, we were left to figure life out together. Though our wedding was exciting, we were unprepared for the intense roller coaster ride ahead. You can never be too ready for marriage, but with the right tools and a commitment to work together, you can be successful. "Marriage stands the test of times when both you and your spouse work towards making things better. And we are tested the most when we face adversities. If you can sail through the adversities as one, as a team, then you have won half the battle." – Unknown

Having a bubbly connection prior to marriage does not necessarily equate to a thriving union. Therefore, it is imperative that one carefully analyses the reason for marriage. It is your "why" that will keep you going when your friends stop shouting. Recognise and confess your faults to each other and embody an environment conducive to conversation free of judgments. Early and recurring detection serves to preserve and empower the union. Don't just ignore your flaws; pursue the cure. Healing begins with acknowledgment. Significant problems emerge from minuscule issues concealed by pretence. Being honest about your weaknesses does not indicate that you're incompetent or your marriage will not work; your honesty will be a vehicle for finding solutions. A successful marriage is one in which the couple continuously and collectively find and implement solutions for prevailing problems. Discuss openly and candidly your fears, value systems, and struggles. The more your partner knows, the more they can support you. Your spouse is your teammate; marriage is a game that requires total honesty.

Before proceeding, do a SWOT analysis:

- What are your strengths (things you are good at)?
- What are your weaknesses (things you struggle with)?
- What opportunities are available to you (who can you talk to when you need support)?
- What are those threats (fears)?

Normalise being vulnerable with each other; speak openly without judgement. Your honesty will promote growth within the union.

Initially we argued about everything from the "squeezing of the toothpaste to when the bed was to be made". At the time of our marriage, I served the armed forces as an infantry soldier and would leave home for long extensive duties. One evening I came home excited but tired after a long stint of work. My wife was excited to see me; she had my favourite meal prepared but before you know it, we were arguing. "Imagine I prepared your dinner, and you allowed it to get cold because you are out there talking". I had stopped to converse briefly with some friends; before you know it was there for about 2 hours. That evening my wife went to bed early; you could tell she was upset. The following morning, I jumped out of my sleep as I felt someone shaking me. "What! What happened? I queried. Get up, I need to make the bed, the faint voice with annoyance responded. "I am not done sleeping yet" I shouted back. "You need to get up because the day is now bright, what kind of soldier are you?" she shouted. I jumped up and grabbed things and decided to go back to work. On my way out I bumped into my father-in-law. I yelled "Now you can have your daughter back because I can't manage her." Relationships can become rocky at times; it is not the experiences that deters the success of the marriage, it is how we handle each situation. Each experience comes with a unique life lesson, be honest with yourself, acknowledge the problem, apologise, and learn from your error. Mr Brown is much shorter in statute but the lessons he teaches are life-impacting. In a still little voice, he said, "communicate Nick, communicate. You are two unique individuals who must keep the airways open for communication. Talk to your wife about your likes and dislikes. Tell her how she can make you happy. Listen to her and act where necessary. Only the two of you can make this relationship work". He patted me on the back and walked away laughing. "To effectively communicate, we must realize that we are all different in the way we perceive the world and use this understanding as a guide to our communication with others." —Tony Robbins

The most effective cure for misunderstanding is communication. It is through this channel we express our desires, clarify misconceptions, and reaffirm trust and love. Both persons come to the relationship with their own experiences, core values, ideas, and practices. If not communicated, they can lead to frequent fracas. Premarital issues, when not addressed early, can have an irreversible impact on a married couple's life.

Everyone has a past, and there is no escaping it. In that past lie memories that are delicate to us. Share these experiences and how they might have affected your life.

Though I was now married, I still struggled with my own unmet desires. Growing up in a home that was characterised by frequent arguing, disrespect, and name-calling affected my self-esteem. I did not consider myself worthy to marry Danielle and thought it would only be a matter of time before everyone else believed the same. I have never seen my parents hug and act lovingly towards each other. I also wrestled with my mom's utterances that I wouldn't be able to make a woman happy.

Release yourself of the baggage so you can grow. Your marriage will never thrive until you discover yourself. Don't just give your spouse a part of you; give them your all. Tell them who you are and what you struggle with. When you do, they will be able to support you better.

I recall going back to discuss it with my wife. At first, it was hard, but it was what was needed to overcome my past so I could excel in my new role as husband. Practise becoming an expert at sharing honestly. Your spouse is not your opponent; he or she is your teammate. Every married couple will hit road bumps in their life together. Some will be easy to overcome with skills and habits of listening and respect, while others will take much time, effort, prayer, and professional help. Marital problems, no matter how simple, must not be ignored. Though we may not be able to solve all problems, we can develop a mechanism to cope and support each other. It is often not the problem that destroys a union but the lack of awareness. Communicating while having disagreements can be difficult, but I want to share with you some tips from my personal collection:

1. reflect on the good times. the presence of great memories is a reminder that union can work. as you reflect, write

down what you did in the past to make your spouse happy.

2. generate a list of all the problems you disagree about. this list may entail things you refrain from sharing because you want to avoid arguing. sometimes, things not discussed can have a more significant impact on the union. pray about them, discuss them, and find amicable solutions. together, you will develop a cheat sheet for managing such conflicts, one that can be implemented again in the future.

3. focus on yourself. oftentimes it is easier to focus on the other person, what they are doing or not doing, and what they need to change. this can cause your spouse to become defensive, allowing the problem to spiral out of control. instead, think about the situation and what you both can do better to make things work. the goal is not to win against your spouse but to win together against the issue.

4. deescalate the problem. when tensions are high, and we feel our needs are not being met, it is easy to say things that will encourage conflict. instead, commit to no more criticism, complaints, blame, accusations, anger, or sarcasm. endeavour to build a positive environment.

5. express your concern constructively. start your thoughts with:

   I feel... [followed by a one-word feeling such as "anxious," "sad," etc.] My concern is...I would like to... [note: NEVER use "I would like you to..."] How would you feel about that? Or what are your thoughts on that?

6. reflect on the marriages of your parents, friends, and community members. every marriage is unique, and you should definitely strive to create a unique recipe for your marriage. the goal is not to become them but to examine their qualities, adopt the good ones, and learn from the bad practices.

7. create a positive environment. do this by hugging, kissing, affirming, and helping more. for every conflict, create beautiful memories. by doing this, you collectively create the anticipation that things will get better after every conflict.

As we practised the tips above, we began to share more fun, loving, and exciting experiences. It isn't the conflict but your will to be more influential than the conflict that matters. Be honest, do the labour, and shut out the noise. Beware of those who make it sound too easy.

I recall asking a minister who was also newly married, "How do you manage conflicts in your relationship?" His response gave us a knock for six. We almost fell into a state of depression as we grappled with questions about what we were doing wrong. He said that everything was perfect. He had never disagreed with his wife. If it sounds too good to be true, then probably it is too good to be true. All marriages experience challenges: what makes the difference is the couple and how they treat disagreements. A thriving marriage involves two people who are skilful at managing conflicts: become one today.

Many times, a person looking from the outside at other people's relationships develops a barrage of wishful desires to have that same kind of 'perfect' relationship, which does not exist because of the deception they allow to infiltrate their perceptions from the facade displayed, especially on social media. Don't just wish to become skilled at managing conflicts.

One day, after another intense disagreement, my father invited Nicholas to help him with some work in the bathroom. Upon entering, he was given broken pliers to unlock a screw on the toilet. Nicholas was so upset that each time he gripped the screw, it slipped off. The broken pliers were ineffective in gripping the area that needed attention, and after a few attempts, he became outraged and threw the tool on the floor. The toilet represented the problems we encountered and the tool, the two of us in the union. My father's wisdom encouraged me to focus on the problem and not the person. It took lessons like these to teach us the value of three critical skills: detect, define, and communicate. While we may know bits and bobs about our partner, it is in the marriage that we will become privy to things packaged too tight for us to recognise prior. Like a detective, we ought to seek to identify what these things are the more we spend time together, especially the nonverbals. After the detection, we must define the matter, and with a name attached, we may meticulously communicate an amicable solution based on our strengths to illuminate the limitations. In this process, we must be careful not to become judgemental but understanding. We listen to understand the wiring of each discovery and, like an electrician, define them before moving to the solution. The longer the wires rub in an incorrect position, the more damaged and expensive it becomes to resolve.

Always remember, the issue is not about the prevailing conflict, but the Modus Operandi used to resolve it. Conflict in marriage is the growth factor; it is an invitation for transformation when both partners apply the lessons learned.

Reflect Now That You Have Proceeded...

Circle the flag light that best describes your assessment of yourself/ partner based on the topic: **Marriage and Problem solving.**

Explain your answer based your previous selection:

Know-Metre: Now appraise your knowledge of this topic after reading by circling the gauge.

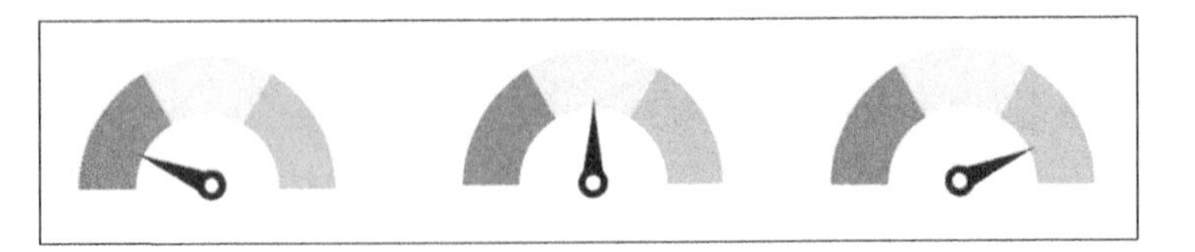

MARRIAGE AND SEXUAL INTIMACY

Nurturing Marital Bliss: Understanding and Cultivating Sexual Intimacy in a Relationship.

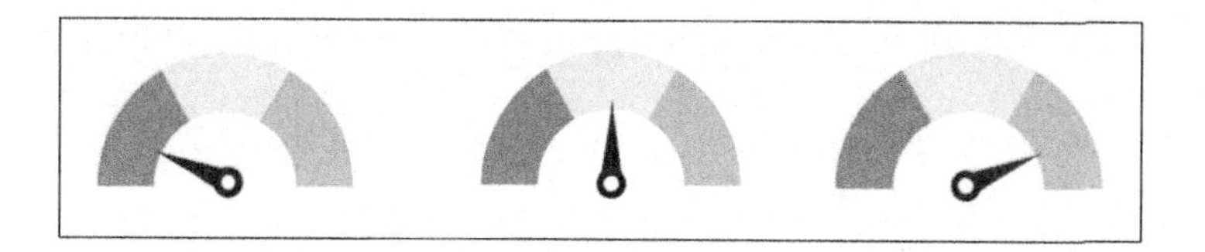

"Couples who know each other intimately [and] are well versed in each other's likes, dislikes, personality quirks, hopes, and dreams are couples who make it." — Dr Gottman

Sex is vital in marriage. It is a crucial ingredient for building intimacy because it creates the space to be vulnerable with one's partner. Sex is a symmetrical exercise that emboldens both partners with the right to excite each other. The couple must immerse themselves entirely into the mission to create a pleasurable moment to achieve maximum benefit. This includes touching, playing with, chewing, or even licking each other in the most sensitive and pleasurable manner. Sexual intimacy begins with believing that you deserve intimacy, sexual pleasure, and connection. This clears your mind of any guilt, shame, or worry, thus allowing you to express your feelings in the most honest and sincere way.

Secondly, sex was created by God to be enjoyed. Therefore, you should be creative in repeatedly exploring your spouse's body, each time hitting all the right spots for ultimate satisfaction. It is evident that with each vicarious orgasm, couples can develop an enchanting bond that helps to strengthen the relationship and arouse pleasure.

Thirdly, you need to believe that sex and sexual pleasure should happen for you and not for anybody else. You are not merely pleasing your partner; you are a primary beneficiary; therefore, invest your all into creating fulfilling and memorable moments. Sex must never be seen as a servicing or tapping-up activity in which you are solely there to provide pleasure to someone else. Rather, it is an activity that you do for yourself. Therefore, don't just have random sexual encounters; plan the scenery, prepare your mind, dress to impress, think about the positions you desire, and immerse your entire being into the moment. Believing that you deserve sexual pleasure and sexual satisfaction in your life is a cornerstone of achieving intimate sex. —Thomas 2016

Fundamental to sexual intimacy is mutual orgasm, that beautiful, rewarding feeling that comes at the end of a good sexual encounter. You must work for it. Research shows that 10-15% of the time, when people do not experience an orgasm, it is caused by tiredness, stress, anxiety, and high alcohol intake. Couples need to take time off from their busy schedules to prepare for maximum sexual pleasure. Leave work early, take leave from work, and create the moment that excites you and your partner. If it means this much to you, it should not be treated as secondary to everything you must do or as a night activity reserved for when the kids are off to sleep. Children should never be used as an excuse. Tuck the kids in early, or get a nanny for a few hours, put a lock on your door, and empower your marriage through sexual intimacy. The most valuable gift you can give your children is modelling a happy and connected relationship. Building intimacy requires effort, time, and commitment.

Fourthly, do not be in such a hurry to get to the finish line. Use your lips, hands, palms, fingers, mouth, teeth, and breasts; every part of your body can give you pleasure. Whereas kissing, hugging, and penetration allow for mutual satisfaction, foreplay is only part of the sexual encounter that will enable partners to take turns to invest in each other's happiness. In each cycle, one partner selflessly puts the other partner at centre stage and meticulously uses all resources available to ensure their partner has the best experience. Foreplay is a signed promise that guarantees results. It promotes feelings that one is desired, aroused, and ready for sex. It encourages partners to look at one another and communicate what feels good through words, hand movements, and noise. Screams, moans, and compliments are incredibly beneficial to the moment. Do not keep quiet when you find that "sweet spot". Feedback is important for future successful experiences; it is making an advance downpayment for tomorrow's satisfaction.

Sexual intimacy can be improved through coaching and guidance. "Yes baby, I like that; give me more. Go harder; yes, yes, slow down, honey."

Be honest but be careful not to discourage your spouse. When one partner becomes critical and aggressive the other will often become defensive and distant. Use positive reinforcement to build your spouse's self-esteem. Rather than saying, "You are not doing it properly", change your position and guide your spouse in how you can best be pleasured.

Dr Gottman in the article "The Science of Trust," opines that expressing a positive need is a recipe for success for both the listener and speaker because it conveys complaints and requests without criticism.

The fundamental for intimate sex is knowing that you deserve the best sexual pleasure, engaging in creative and memorable foreplay, achieving orgasm, scheduling time, planning great sexual encounters, and exploring your partner thoroughly. This can hold your bond together during stressful and complicated seasons in your marriage. It is vital to Learn how to have a deep connection and more intimacy with your partner, as this will protect the relationship and keep your bond strong.

Sex is pure and should be seen as a ministry, an occasion to serve each other. It should never be ignored or denied for reasons beyond consent. The first-century writer Paul, in his first letter to the Corinthians, admonished his audience to refrain from withholding sex for any reason other than which the partner consents as your body is the possession of your partner.

"So do not withhold *sex* from one another unless both of you have agreed to devote a certain period of time to prayer. When the agreed time is over, come together again so that Satan will not tempt you when you are short on self-control." — 1 Corinthians 7:5 (The Voice).

Paul strongly puts forth the idea that there is a mutual sexual responsibility in marriage. The husband has obligations toward his wife, and the wife has obligations toward her husband. An investment into your spouse's pleasure brings reciprocal benefits. Do not miss out on opportunities for meaningful excitement. In a marriage characterized by mutual love, we have a binding obligation to serve our partner with physical and sexual affection. Create an atmosphere where sex is enjoyed. Of the billion-plus people in the world, you have been handpicked and endowed with the tremendous responsibility to serve your spouse sexually. Do everything honourable to satisfy your spouse's needs.

In the letter, Paul makes it clear that there is nothing wrong with married couples engaging in good and meaningful sex; rather, everything is right about sexual pleasure and sex in marriage. Satan's intent, when it comes to sex, is to do everything he can to encourage sex outside of marriage and to discourage sex within marriage. It is an equal victory for Satan if he accomplishes either plan.

When married couples wilfully deny each other sex, they excite God's enemy while denying God the glory and making their spouse unhappy. Do everything in your power to make the enemy mad. Do it frequently and passionately. Neither husband nor wife should accept a poor sexual relationship. Problems may never be eliminated from your union but serve each other sexually. God wants every Christian marriage to enjoy a sexual relationship. It is His special blessing reserved for married people.

Many persons enter marriage with high anticipation that sex will be frequent. The reality is that if we do not fan the flames, we may experience differing seasons; some seasons, you will have lots of sex, some little sex, and others just enough. Discern the seasons and implement the appropriate measures to improve the sexual climate. These measures include communicating, complementing, and comforting. During seasons of tension, sexual expressions tend to decline in both quantity and quality. Do everything in your might to resolve conflicts quickly and boost sexual passion. Remember, we must enjoy sex; you deserve to, and your spouse is depending on you.

Keep the opponent frustrated. Engage in hot, planned, spontaneous, quality, and frequent sex for maximum intimacy.

Sexual intimacy can be enhanced by reigniting the flames through fresh and innovative experiences. Passionate and personal encounters are the outcome of the magnetic bonding between two adventurous people stemming from the high volumes of dopamine released in the brain. This neurotransmitter is heightened by the physical attraction and romantic passion shared by the couple, often sparking significant arousal. Touch that special place, talk sexy to each other, hold each other, and create a sexually conducive environment. "Without attachment, a naked body is merely a lifeless sex-toy." — Abhijit Naska

The more you explore your partner's body, the more you can identify their likes, dislikes, and sexual preferences. Foster an action plan to increase the serving of their likes, reduce or eliminate those dislikes, and, most importantly, overdose them with those preferences. Serving your partner's interest is an investment into a lifetime of happiness. Make your service unique; this will keep your spouse yearning for more. Always add a special to the menu and provide a special treat when pleased with the service. Here are some ideas for a special treat:

1) Plan a sexy getaway night

Crafting a memorable getaway night for your spouse involves the delicate art of anticipation and thoughtful planning. Begin by considering your partner's preferences, whether it's a cozy cabin retreat, a seaside escape, or a cultural city adventure. Tailor the evening to include elements that resonate with shared experiences and interests. Arrange surprises, such as a favourite meal, a nostalgic activity, or perhaps a scenic spot to stargaze. Pay attention to the small details, from ambient lighting to a carefully curated playlist, fostering an atmosphere that exudes romance and relaxation. The key lies in thoughtful gestures that reflect your deep understanding of your spouse, creating a getaway night that becomes a cherished chapter in your shared story.

2) Incorporate role playing

Become all things good and moral to serve your partner's interest. Role-playing can be planned or spontaneous, but planned ones can be even more fulfilling, so invest some time in preparation. As you plan that sexy role-play play, think about the following:

- The characters and their roles.
- The back story that will give life to the plot.
- The ideal costumes to immerse yourself into the setting.
- The time and choice of scene.

Ensure you choose something you are both familiar with or simply research.

Now that you have everything you need, dress up and have fun. Give it your all. At the end of each experience, remember that feedback is vital to ongoing success.

3) Create a class

Teamwork requires the full cooperation of its members. Discuss your needs and fantasies, research, and practise for perfection. Create an atmosphere of continuous learning to foster sexual growth and development.

4) Plan sex "information finding night"

Good results require thorough and meaningful investigation. Your partner has a lot to say on the matter of sex; create an atmosphere that makes it easy to discuss sex and unleash your spouse's expertise.

5) Include music

Watch a hot romantic movie or listen to some provocative music to thrust into the moment of sexual connection.

6) Take centre stage and pleasure yourself

This can be very tempting and create a never-ending thirst and hunger for your tantalising body. Allowing your partner to witness you touch, play with, and pleasure yourself in the most vulnerable manner encourages proximity and trust. It provides vital details about how you are to be handled.

7) **Model your passion**

If you want to be slapped, grabbed, choked, or kissed deeply, model this. Do unto others as you would like them to do unto you.

.

Do not allow anything to deter you from enjoying a moment of titillating erotic rendezvous. Know the signs of "intimacy decliners", act quickly to enjoy continuous pleasure, and maintain a mouth-watering experience through quality bonding. Several things can reduce the desire for sex, such as disappointment, stress, and unhappiness. Take care not to belittle your partner during these instances of low seasons. Instead, communicate, forgive, and ramp up the serving. Cease every opportunity to excite your spouse sexually. Today is an excellent time to sharpen your passion and create a "swaggerific" experience. Make your home sex friendly.

Conflicts can develop from thoughts of insecurity, internal and mental struggles, dissatisfaction with one's appearance, and the frequent comparisons we make, whether that is comparing ourselves or our spouses with others. Be open and thoughtful and share how you really feel. Take steps to reduce friction and build bridges of harmony in your relationship. A moment of tranquilizing sexual pleasure can be useful to boost your confidence and renew your passion for each other. So, choose a suitable and convenient setting, perhaps over a glass of "red wine" decked out in the most sexy and exotic outfit, rocking or dancing to soothing audio while holding each other close and steering into each other's eyes. Understanding the seasons is equally important as the sexual activity itself. Do not only address the sex; fix the climate to enjoy lasting sexual pleasure. Send a sexy text from work to create anticipation, engage your spouse in "fiery" sexting, and create and share unusual challenges to create lasting memories. Memories can be therapeutic.

Observe keenly and learn your partner's love language. Your partner is unique and different from everyone else. Invest time to know what turns them on and off. Failing to address these needs can be catastrophic and has the potential to affect your sexual intimacy. Learn to communicate honestly yet wisely. Rather than emphasising what we do not like, accentuate the things they do appreciate. Focusing on our likes lets our partner wheel the desired romance in motion. Remember to communicate. If ineffective, we should try to be more direct but not defensive in voicing our desires.

While we do not anticipate an extensive 'no sex season,' health issues and hormonal changes can sometimes prevent sexual interaction but should not eliminate total intimacy. Intimacy is not limited to sex; instead, sex is an essential tool for intimacy. We can magnify sexual intimacy without realizing the need for intellectual, spiritual, emotional, and social intimacy, all of which are critical to bonding.

Finally, Terry Gaspard's article "10 Ways to Rekindle The Passion In Your Marriage" suggests that the ensuing tips are useful for building lasting intimacy.

1. Change the way you initiate sex

Find new and more innovative ways to practice sexual intimacy. Use a variety of mediums that you and your spouse are comfortable with. Make every experience count.

2. **Hold hands frequently**

Holding hands, hugging, and touching regularly can release oxytocin, causing one to become calm, relaxed, and sexually excited, and can lead to high volumes of sexual orgasm. Physical affection also reduces stress hormones and promotes a more pleasurable experience.

3. **Build tension and stimulate interest**

Our brains experience more pleasure when the anticipation of the reward goes on for some time before we receive it. So, take your time during foreplay, share fantasies, change locations, and make sex more romantic.

4. **Separate sexual encounters from regular routines**

Plan intimacy time and avoid talking about relationship problems and household chores in the bedroom. Sexual arousal plummets when we're distracted and stressed.

5. **Set aside time to spend with your spouse**

Try a variety of activities that bring you both pleasure. Have fun courting and practice flirting to ignite sexual desire and intimacy. Dr. Gottman says, "everything positive you do in your relationship is foreplay."

6. Practice touching affectionately

Offer to rub your partner's back or shoulder. People associate foreplay with sexual intercourse, but affectionate touch is a powerful way to demonstrate and rekindle passion, even if you are not a touchy-feely person.

7. Be emotionally vulnerable during sex

Share your innermost wishes, fantasies, and desires with your partner. If you fear emotional intimacy, consider engaging in individual or couple's therapy.

8. Be curious about sexual intimacy

Try new ways to bring pleasure to each other through sex. Let your senses come alive while stimulating sexual interest. The entire body is carefully designed with nerves that, if tasted, sucked, touched, caressed, or massaged, can become a complete system of sexual chemistry. Vary your sex appetite as this is an opportunity to get to know your partner better over time.

9. Have different kind of sex

Have gentle, loving-tender, intimate, and highly erotic sex. Break up the routine and try new things as sexual needs change.

10. Prioritise sex

Set the mood for intimacy before sitting down to watch the television as work dulls your passion. A light meal along with your favourite music and wine, can set the stage for great sex. Remember, even if you are not a touchy-feely person, increasing physical affection and emotional attunement can help you sustain a deep, meaningful bond.

Dear couple,

Now that you have read this chapter on sexual intimacy, we would like to invite you on a journey to 21 Days of Shades and SexEd Revolutionised. Get these books and join the tour for brighter and even greater sexual encounters.

Reflect Now That You Have Proceeded…

Circle the flag light that best describes your assessment of yourself/ partner based on the topic: **Marriage and Sexual Intimacy.**

Explain your answer based your previous selection:

Know-Metre: Now appraise your knowledge of this topic after reading by circling the gauge.

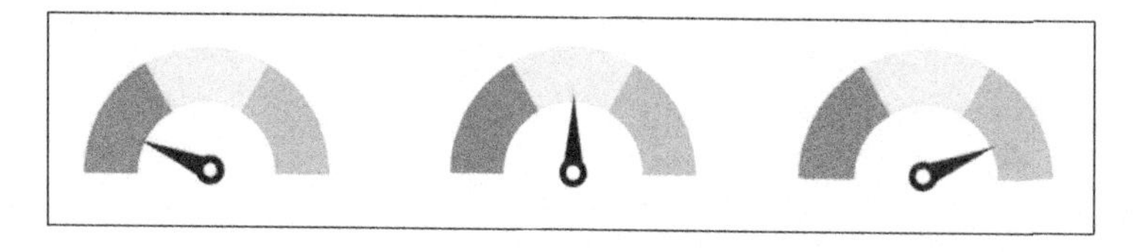

MARRIAGE AND RESILIENCE

Thriving Together: Cultivating Resilience in Marriage Through Challenges and Transitions.

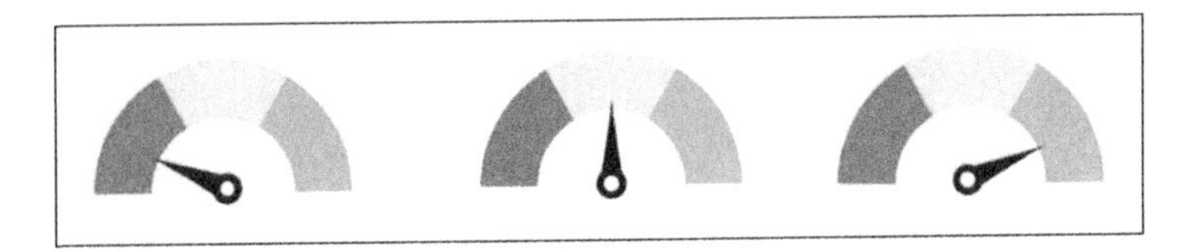

"Your marriage will not be defined by the size of your struggles, but by the size of your commitment to overcome those struggles together." – Dave Willis

I get it, "marriage is hard work". Sometimes, it is the very reason for the ongoing pain, discomfort, and anger that you feel deep inside. Marriage has the propensity to cause you to feel trapped within inescapable and fortified prison walls. It is perfectly normal to feel like packing your bags and escaping to a place of no return. Early into our marriage, there were days we wondered if our union was under a curse. We had conflict after conflict instantaneously, frequently, and abundantly. Going through a day without some "silly" disagreement was almost impossible. Our arguments stemmed from very basic and everyday issues. What made it unbelievable all the most was that we rarely had disagreements during our dating and courting seasons.

We tried compromising, a popular advice often given by relationship gurus. However, the results were often short-lived because it is trifling for any individual to deny their interest at the expense of making another person happy. Compromising can be selfish and self-serving, sometimes creating a buffer that only temporarily addresses the issue. Conflicts and disagreements can be a good teacher of self and a revealer of things that need to be addressed, thus creating new experiences. On that account, compromising limits creativity and robs the couple of an opportunity to learn more about each other. A desire that always attempts to be fair and equitable may unintentionally affect the result. In most relationships, couples employ this strategy to avoid addressing the real needs, replacing more lasting resolutions with temporary peace of mind. Whenever we argued, I avoided discussing the real problem and how it made me feel by compensating my wife with a small gift or kiss. This would bring about a moment of joy; however, it would not be enough to last a lifetime. There was something to discuss, but we covered it rather than taking steps to heal the wound. The truth is neither of us leaves the negotiating table completely happy. We simply did what was necessary to keep going for a short time. Ultimately, this becomes a recurring theme as similar conflict often occurs in the future. Some people want to remain married but are unwilling to do the work that comes with being married.

Some years ago, after living abroad, we returned home for a short stint. Our house was totally unrecognisable. Grass covered the driveway, while wasps and other insects took residence on our house structure. Getting to the veranda without getting wet in the dew was almost impossible. How did our home reach that deplorable condition? After migrating, we could not get a caretaker to maintain the property, so the property was left unkept. It was a lovely home, but it needed to be maintained. The differences were obvious as we stood by the roadway gazing into our neighbour's yard. Their home was well kept; beautiful lawn, well painted, and nicely arranged. We became a bit "jealous," wishing our home was the same or better. But simply wishing is not enough; we must be committed to work. Moments later, the answer to our query became apparent. A slim, tall man appeared outside with tools and began to work on his landscape. This is the exact difference between successful marriages and those ending in divorce. Soon after, a beautiful short lady appeared with some drinks and snacks. The success of every marriage depends on the willpower of the partners in the union to collaborate. It was no one else's responsibility to ensure the home was taken care of.

Similarly, God is not responsible for making your relationship work. As a loving Father, He equipped you with the manual to inspire success. You must read, understand, and apply it (work) to maximise your chance of having a successful relationship. Ask yourself why Muslims and other unbelievers' marriages are working. Successful marriages are the culmination of the dedication of people willing to apply the principles taught in scripture to make the marriage work. God will help you make the right choices and give you wisdom and strength, but He will not apologise to your spouse for you or express appreciation on your behalf. You are the primary stakeholder in your marriage; take the lead and build a successful union. At that moment, we decided to get to work, sourcing lawn grass, weeding and removing garbage, and planting trees. In a few months, our home began to look like the home next door. Stop staring at your neighbour's marriage and start working on your union. Every union is a seed that can grow; however, growing depends on the will of the stakeholders to work.

We must commit to harnessing the reliance necessary to create healthy and happy marriages. Working in a marriage involves learning, developing, and applying strategies to ensure the union progresses. Marriage can be a beautiful experience, providing love, support, and companionship. However, like anything else worth having, marriage is not stress-free and requires effort and attention. Below are some tips for building resilience in your union:

Pray together

Prayer yields instructions on how to proceed in marriage. When you pray, you must be ready to carry out the directives God gives. (Solomon, Proverbs 3:5,6) "*Trust God from the bottom of your heart; don't try to figure out everything on your own. Listen for God's voice in everything you do, everywhere you go; he's the one who will keep you on track.*"

Work together

Remember you are a team; a failure for one is a failure for both. Studies show that the more the couple engages and works together, the more likely the unit will develop a close bond, grow in love, and develop a sincere appreciation for each other. In essence, a couple that sweat together is likelier to stay together. Additional research shows that couples who are active and supportive of each other's pursuits are generally happier. Working together fortifies their emotional, mental, psychological, and physical bond. Additionally, each partner becomes the other's built-in accountability partner to inspire and motivate.

Be still and relax

Sometimes, a moment of stillness can be extremely valuable in helping you reset your thoughts and make wise choices. Discussions with several couples suggest that when they are tired/overwhelmed, they become easily angry and usually say things they later regret. Therefore, take frequent breaks to unwind and release the adrenaline and cortisol. Some activities are prayer and meditation, a quiet walk in the park, reflection and journaling, affirmations, or a daily relaxation exercise such as a simple breathing technique. This can empower you physiologically and psychologically. Our world is quite fast-paced, and often, we get caught up in the demanding schedules that we forget to take care of each other. Look out for your spouse and plan moments for just relaxing. Choose the right time and place for your most serious conversations. When our stress response kicks inclines, our relaxation response helps us to cope.

Express gratitude regularly

Studies increasingly show that frequent shows of appreciation can improve physical and psychological health, enhance the ability to empathise with others, reduce aggression, improve self-esteem, and create a bond between each other. Stress, depression, and other life challenges can cause us to forget the many things we are to be grateful for, including our spouse and the efforts they make to make us happy. Make a deliberate attempt every day to acknowledge and share the things you are most grateful for. Practise saying, "Hun, I appreciate your constant support, your willingness always to listen, and thanks for the healthy meal you prepared today." You can also implement this daily gratitude practice by writing down what you're grateful for or simply sharing it at the dinner table.

Begin your statement with, "Today I am most grateful for…". Gratitude is the opposite of complaining or reporting the faults you notice. It is much easier to complain than it is to compliment. Beating down on your spouse is the most effective way to end your marriage. Not only will it make both of you miserable, but research shows that all the extra cortisol released by frequent complaining impairs your immune system and makes you more susceptible to high cholesterol, diabetes, heart disease, and obesity. It even makes the brain more vulnerable to strokes. Sometimes, the easiest way to prompt someone to improve is to acknowledge what they are excelling at. At some point in our marriage, we were stark complainers. "You didn't do this", "You forgot this", "I am the only one who has to do this". Often, a moment of selfish complaining causes you to forget what the other person does to help the union. One spouse may go out to work and navigate the challenges at work, which sometimes can be overwhelming, whereas the other spouse spends time preparing meals, maintaining the residence, and caring for the children. Complaining can be selfish and paints the picture of one perfect human being doing everything right with a horrible partner who makes no effort to support. There is a place for both persons to talk about how they feel. However, the results may prove better if one begins with "GRATEFULNESS." A will to recognise gratitude means that you are deliberately removing the spotlight from yourself, the 'perfect being', and looking through the lens of compassion at your spouse to acknowledge even the simplest good they do make your home and lives together better.

Using the "What Went Well" model can help guide your reflection.

Guidance: Reflect briefly on all your spouse does daily and make a note of what you are grateful for.

What Went Well

Forgive quickly

In the intricate dance of marriage, the ability to forgive quickly emerges as a foundation for a resilient and thriving partnership. The nature of human interactions within matrimony inevitably invites moments of misunderstanding, disagreement, or unintentional hurt. Embracing the art of swift forgiveness becomes a potent antidote to resentment, allowing couples to navigate through the inevitable rough patches with grace. Choosing to forgive promptly not only nurtures emotional well-being but also fosters an environment where empathy and understanding can flourish. It's a conscious decision that acknowledges the imperfections inherent in any relationship, steering the course towards harmony and lasting connection.

Sleep together

The temptation is to isolate from each other during conflicts. This response to conflict only escalates the problem and extends the period of unhappiness. Sleeping together is a reminder that at the end of the day literally or figuratively speaking, both of you will need to resolve the conflict. Develop the discipline to:

- pray together before bed,
- converse before bed
- wish each other well before you go off to sleep.

Marriage is a gift; many people long to be married. Maximise your marriage to the full extent.

Set goals together

The success of a marriage requires clear and shared focus. Therefore, the couple should endeavour to create meaningful targets and milestones to achieve their overall goal and develop practical steps to arrive at actualisation. By setting goals together, the couple can focus their energy in a single direction. As you work toward your goals, you can hold each other accountable and provide encouragement to help you each succeed.

Know the warning signs of your spouse's stress response

It is important to understand your own and your partner's unique responses to stress. What warning signs do you start seeing when stressed out? Are there physical signs such as clenching their jaw or balling their fists? Are there behavioural changes, such as getting short, snippy, or compulsively list-making? Whatever they are, paying attention and simply being aware can make you more sensitive to their needs and be a better support system.

Reflect Now That You Have Proceeded...

Circle the flag light that best describes your assessment of yourself/ partner based on the topic: **Marriage and Resilience.**

Explain your answer based your previous selection:

Know-Metre: Now appraise your knowledge of this topic after reading by circling the gauge.

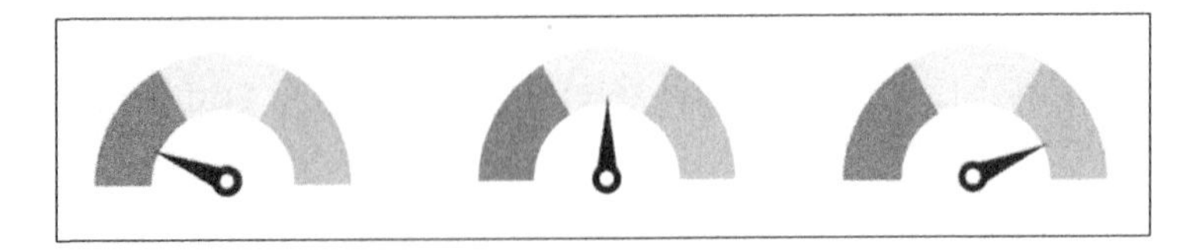

MARRIAGE AND LAUGHTER

The Importance of Laughter in Marriage: Fostering Joy, Resilience, and Connection.

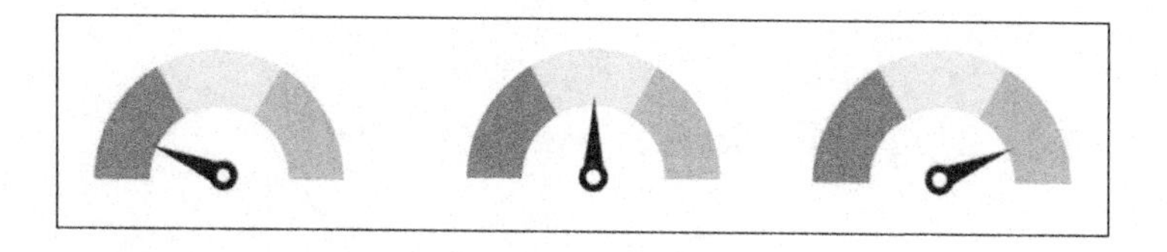

"Laughter is best medicine." — Unknown

A couple that laughs together will keep the wrinkles and fusses away. Make it your duty to laugh with your spouse daily. This may include finding a funny video or work of art or just making fun of some everyday activities. If you want to score big, try laughing at inside jokes only the two of you share. This has proven to have significant health benefits for people in both the long and short term.

Laughter not only lightens your load mentally, but it induces physical changes in your body, such as:

Stimulating several organs

Frequent bouts of laughter enhance oxygen intake, stimulate the heart, lungs, and muscles, and increase the endorphins released by the brain.

Activating and relieving stress response

An exuberant laughter stimulates your stress response, thus impacting your heart rate and blood pressure, which results in a feeling characterised by relaxation.

Soothing tension

Laughter can revive circulation and help with muscle relaxation, which together can reduce stress and anxiety.

Improving your immune system

Research shows that negative thoughts can result in the release of chemical reactions that can affect your body by increasing stress and anxiety at the same time, reducing immunity. On the other hand, positive thoughts release neuropeptides that help to combat stress and potentially more serious illnesses.

Relieving pain

It is believed that regular moments of laughter can ease pain, causing the body to produce its own natural painkillers called endorphins. These endorphins bind to opioid receptors in the brain to deter the perception of pain. The more you laugh, the more likely you are to develop these natural hormones, which can substantially help reduce the physical pain you feel from illnesses and produce profound feelings of pleasure and satisfaction.

Increasing personal satisfaction

Laughter makes functioning in and handling difficult situations easier, and a pleasant attitude reduces friction. In an article entitled "Laughter Therapy May Increase Life Satisfaction, Study Finds," Sarah Feilding opines that "laughter helps to provide human connection and emotional bonding and is one of the most powerful tools against depression and loneliness."

Building social bonds

Laughter will help you connect with other people.

Improve your mood.

Several people experience depression largely because of chronic illnesses. Laughter can help lessen stress, depression, and anxiety and may make you feel happier. It can also improve your self-esteem. "Laughter helps to provide human connection and emotional bonding and is one of the most powerful tools against depression and loneliness."- Jenna Pascual. Creating scenes of laughter is an effective way to build resilience in marriage. The happier and more welcoming you are, the happier your spouse will be. Invest in your laughter and happiness and create an environment conducive to love and affection. Be the lead entertainer in your relationship, smile regularly, and enjoy a happy and healthy union. You may ponder, "But what if I am not funny enough, or I just do not have a humorous attitude at all?" The good news is that laughter can be perfected.

Here are a few tips for improving your sense of humour:

- **Make humour a priority**

Find some items that will help you laugh, such as photos, greeting cards or comic strips, memes, videos, comedy movies, TV shows, books, magazines, funny websites, and humorous podcasts. You can also attend a comedy club or stand-up comedy show. Be sure to share these experiences with your spouse.

- **Model laughing**

It is believed that if you laugh, the world will laugh with you. Therefore, develop a way to laugh about your own experiences and, at the same time, watch your own stress fade. It may feel forced at first but keep practising as laughter will have a lasting impact on you and your spouse. Laughter creates a happy environment.

- **Be kind; share your laughter**

Create regular opportunities to share laughter with your spouse by sharing something you found funny or just by staring at your spouse and smiling.

Dear couple,

Marriage and laughter share an inseparable bond, intertwining to create a tapestry of joy and resilience within the fabric of a relationship. Laughter acts as a symphony, composing moments of lightness and warmth amid the complexities of marriage. It's the melodious rhythm that punctuates the mundane, transforming ordinary instances into cherished memories. Shared laughter becomes the glue that binds partners together, fostering connection, understanding, and an unspoken language that transcends words. It serves as a beacon during stormy times, infusing hope, and reminding couples of the strength found in shared mirth. Within the laughter exchanged lies a treasure trove of inside jokes, playful banter, and the simple pleasure of finding joy in each other's presence, painting the canvas of married life with vibrant hues of happiness and togetherness.

Reflect Now That You Have Proceeded...

Circle the flag light that best describes your assessment of yourself/ partner based on the topic: **Marriage and Laughter.**

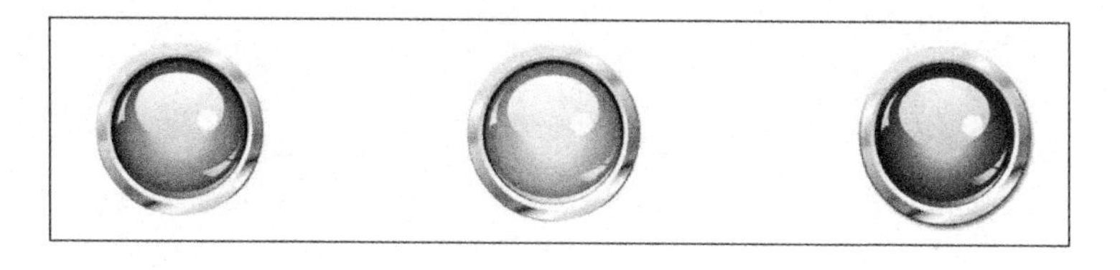

Explain your answer based your previous selection:

Know-Metre: Now appraise your knowledge of this topic after reading by circling the gauge.

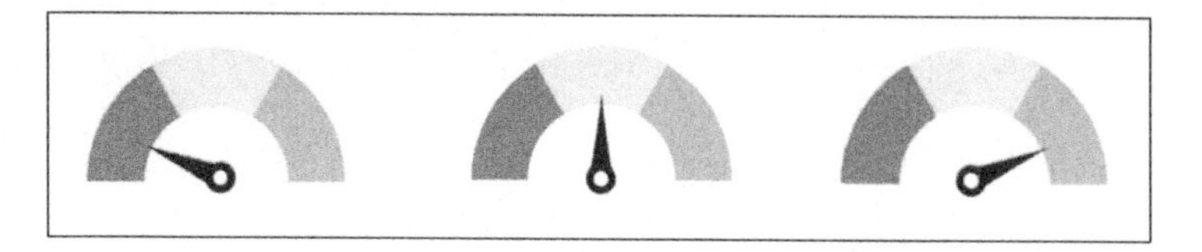

MARRIAGE AND LISTENING

The Art of Active Listening in Marriage: Building Stronger Connections Through Communications.

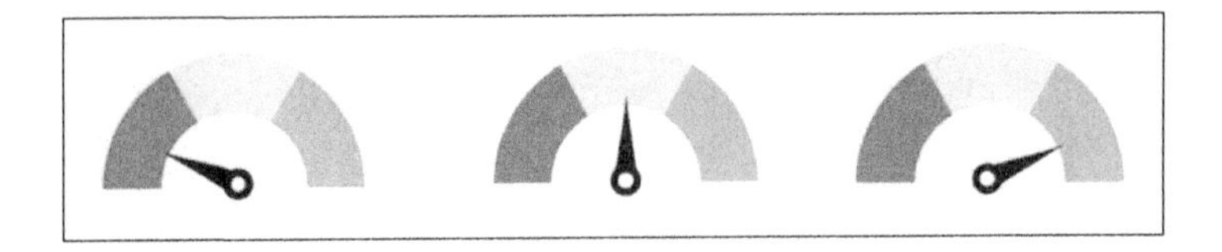

Listening to your partner and trying to understand their perspective is a keyway to show respect in your relationship.
— Unknown

Earlier in our marriage, Danielle and I were strong debaters. Of course, what would you expect? I served my entire college years debating politics and matters of faith. My passion was to always be "right". On the other hand, my wife was a passionate law student; she did not believe in backing down. She was going to state her points firmly and search diligently for the details to support her arguments. These skills were adopted quickly into our marriage and applied even to the slightest disagreement. Sometimes, we were passionate about getting our points across with little interest in the impact it would have on the other person. One day, after an intense showdown that left both of us wounded, our father attempted to guide us into reflection. "Someone has to bell the cat", he stated emphatically. This was his way of explaining to us that someone had to take the responsibility to listen carefully. Listening is an awesome opportunity to serve your spouse, promote their interest, and validate their feelings. In a discussion, especially one characterised by passion, it can be easier to shout several responses rather than listen to our spouse and validate their thoughts. We must, therefore, make a deliberate attempt to listen to each other. It is through listening that we will improve the quality of our communication, thus promoting healthy unions. The rising tension can mar abilities to listen carefully, emphatically, and patiently. Therefore, the art of listening must be developed and, in some cases, taught.

When you actively listen, even in the heat of a disagreement, you build trust and intimacy with your partner. ¬ Unknown

Oftentimes, we get caught up in what we have to say, what we feel, and what we think and fail to listen to how our partner feels. It's so easy to become selfish and make the conversation about our own feelings, but it's critical that we strive to become good listeners. Listening gives us an opportunity to highlight and serve our spouse's needs.

One of the sincerest forms of respect is actually listening to what another has to say. - Bryant H. McGill

This chapter seeks to help readers develop an understanding of active listening, its benefits, and its application. Of course, it sounds easy: just stop talking and listen to what your spouse has to say. But is it really?

Danielle and I quickly learned that being intelligent does not mean we know how to listen effectively. Often, we would interrupt each other or abruptly end the conversation by offering our own solutions. Other times, we delayed listening to address what we deemed to be more urgent activities. Relationships must be other-centred. It is all about trying to serve each other selflessly and lovingly. Listening reinforces your commitment to support each other continuously.

“The first duty of love is to listen.” — Paul Tillich

Listening is not the same as hearing. However, spouses constantly confuse the two. We can hear something we genuinely have no interest in or intent to act upon. Therefore, hearing is merely the process, function, or power to perceive sounds. Listening, on the other hand, means “to pay attention to sound; to hear something with thoughtful attention; and to give consideration.” Couples who excel at marriage are those who can hone their ability to listen. In a conversation, the goal is not merely to perceive your spouse’s voice but to pay attention.

Listening may be passive or active. Passive listening occurs when the listener has no intention of contributing to the conversation; therefore, it is not the most useful type of listening. Sometimes, a spouse feels it is better to just listen to what the other is saying with no real desire to contribute because of the perception that sharing any information can lead to disagreement. Active listening means we patiently pay attention and respond to our spouse to improve mutual understanding and reduce friction. Furthermore, it shows that we are willing to suspend our own concerns, needs, and thoughts temporarily so we can give our full attention to our partner as we seek to devise meaning of the words, tone of voice, and body language. As we pay attention, we will develop an understanding of our spouse's need and the issue of concern and thus become resourceful in helping them think of a working solution. It is important to understand that as the listener, you are facilitating the conversation, not advising unless requested.

"While we might perceive ourselves as being helpful by giving instructions or explaining how to do something, our partner might interpret this behaviour as us always needing to be right." — Gaspard, 2020

Such misunderstanding can create more difficulty for the union by expanding the issue. Your suggestions or opinions may be correct, but it is worth asking yourself:

- Do I want to be right, or do I want us to be happy?

Every act within your union must be undertaken with a selfless drive to make each other happy. Do everything in your might to promote happiness in your union. Listening to your spouse carefully is a small price to pay for continuous bonding.

"In marriage, each partner is to be an encourager rather than a critic, a forgiver rather than a collector of hurts, an enabler rather than a reformer." — Wright and Oliver

The couple can learn to listen actively by baring the ensuing considerations in mind:

Adopt the appropriate posture

Our posture communicates our interest and genuine care for our spouse. At the same time, we want our spouse to feel comfortable; thus, our posture can help create a conducive environment for communication. To do this, maintain an open stance that will ensure you do not cross your arms and legs, as this creates a closed posture, insinuating one is uninterested in what is being discussed. It also shows that you are defensive. For better results, sit slightly forward or lean slightly sideward. That assures your spouse that you are listening and care about what you are listening to. Also, try tilting your head towards your spouse or placing your head on your hands if facing each other.

Turn to your spouse and look straight into their eyes

At first, this will feel somewhat uncomfortable, but if you practise, you will perfect the art. Practice looking into your partner's eyes for about three (3) minutes without being distracted. Try not to make your partner uncomfortable by staring directly at them; for better results, turn your body at an angle to avoid causing your spouse to feel vulnerable. The goal is to support, not intimidate. This tells your spouse that you are extremely interested in what they must share.

Pay attention

Just because you are staring does not mean you are attentive. The goal of effective listening is to create a conducive environment for your spouse to think and share comfortably. Observe verbal and nonverbal communications keenly and know when to allow time for reflection before responding. Please do not cut your spouse off or attempt to silence them. Listening gives you an opportunity to promote your partner's interest through acts of selfless service. Avoid completing their sentences or formulating responses before they are finished. Reflect on your own body language and your frame of mind before engaging in listening. Sometimes, a bad day or low season can affect how you see. Your partner is counting on you; do it as if your marriage depends on it. Remain focused and give your undivided attention. Listening is an opportunity to show attention to your spouse and what he or she cares about. Listening to your partner and trying to understand their perspective is a keyway to show respect in your relationship." — Unknown

Be Open minded

Listen without casting judgments or forming conclusions. Your spouse needs the freedom to express themselves, even if what is being said makes you uncomfortable or disturbed. Do not interrupt. Reflect on what is being said and avoid mounting a defence. Listen with the intent to learn what your spouse cares about. It is normal to have strong views, but in this moment, suspend any judgement, withhold criticisms, and avoid arguing. Remember, your responsibility is to listen carefully to your spouse.

Clarify

Ask questions to:

- confirm that what you heard is what was shared.
- gain greater insight into your spouse's needs.

It is more useful to ask open-ended, clarifying, and probing questions that will encourage your spouse to actively engage in self-reflection and problem-solving rather than justifying or defending a position or trying to guess the "right answer." A good listener helps his or her partner to generate solutions. Examples of probing open-ended questions include: "What do you think about ...?" or "Tell me about ...?" and "Will you further explain/describe ...?"

The emphasis of active listening is on asking instead of telling. This invites a thoughtful response and maintains a spirit of collaboration.

Summarise

As you listen attentively, restate themes during the conversation to boost your understanding. This clears up misunderstandings and allows your spouse to provide further explanation if needed.

▪ Share

Your Spouse shares because he or she wants to be heard and understood. Therefore, the overall goal is for you first to gain an understanding of your partner and his or her needs and, secondly, to communicate effectively so that you can be understood. A good understanding of your partner's perspective will help you develop new ideas and suggestions, show compassion, make changes, or reassure your spouse of your love and support. Continue to engage your spouse in conversation by asking questions to trigger his or her comments. As you ask, make suggestions where necessary; do not dictate the solution. Show empathy where you were wrong and take responsibility. Keep in mind that repentance must be followed up with action. Demonstrate understanding of your spouse's discomfort by apologising genuinely.

Dear couple,

In the symphony of marriage, listening is the quiet but powerful conductor, orchestrating harmony and understanding between partners. It's the art of truly hearing not just the words spoken, but the emotions, fears, and dreams behind them. Listening in marriage is an act of empathy, creating a sacred space where each partner feels heard, valued, and understood. It involves attentive ears and an open heart, ready to embrace the vulnerabilities and complexities of sharing a life. Through listening, couples build bridges of trust and compassion, cultivating a deep connection that weaves their stories together, allowing them to navigate the ebbs and flows of life's journey hand in hand, knowing they are heard and cherished.

Great marriages involve two great listeners; make yours phenomenal by listening frequently to each other.

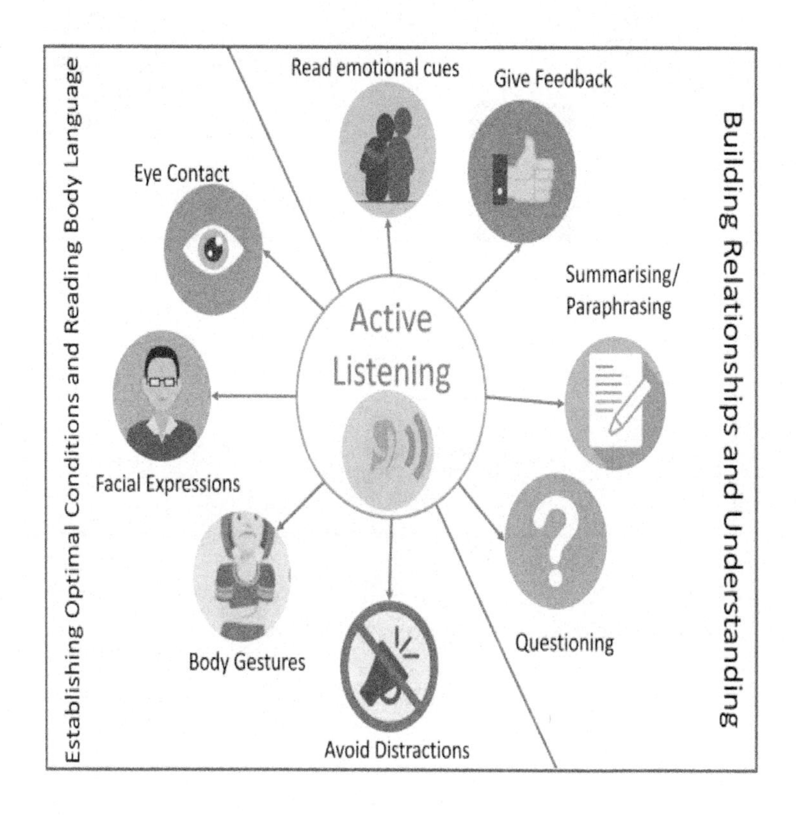

Reflect Now That You Have Proceeded…

Circle the flag light that best describes your assessment of yourself/ partner based on the topic: **Marriage and Listening.**

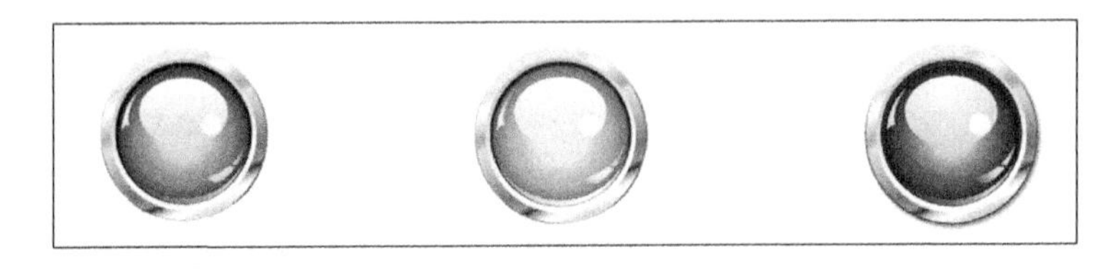

Explain your answer based your previous selection:

Know-Metre: Now appraise your knowledge of this topic after reading by circling the gauge.

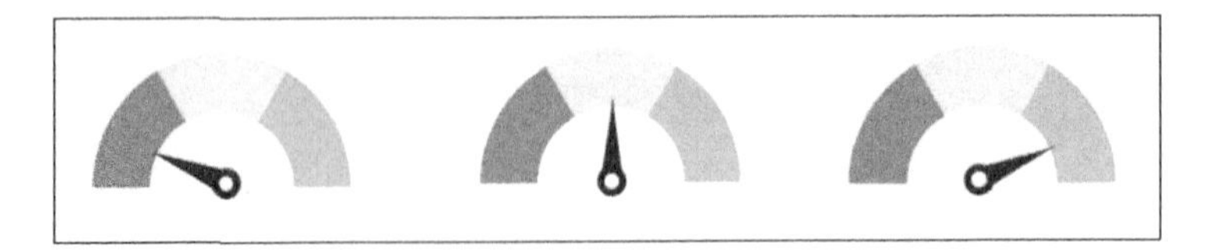

MARRIAGE, GRUDGES AND STONEWALLING

Exploring the Impact of Stonewalling in Marital Relationships: Causes, Consequences, and Strategies for Healthy Relationships.

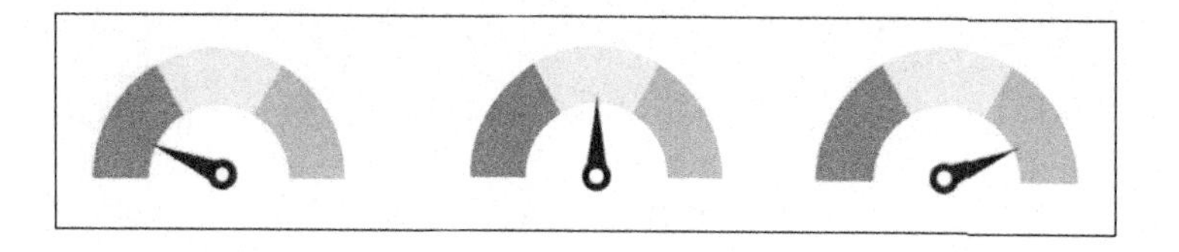

"A great marriage is not when the *'perfect couple'* come together. It is when an imperfect couple learns to enjoy their differences." — Dave Meur

"A healthy partnership flourishes with open and healthy communication, where both partners are respectful." - unknown. Everyone dreams of a marriage free of disagreements, filled with love and compassion, one in which they rise with the sun to a delectable breakfast in bed after a healthy serving of "hot and spicy" sex, with a dash of oral delight. One in which partners are devoted to their faith in God and selflessly honour each other. Borne out of excellent communication and undying attraction, a marriage characterised by appreciation and continuous hunger for each other, a space where the couple delight in each other and is never tired of the different taste that engulfs the frame of their body with the propensity to create heaven on earth after a storm. The institute of love and eternal communion, studying, understanding, and exploring the erotic zones, constantly spotting new havens for emerging and exciting elation, always stimulating each other's interest. Unfortunately, as much as this is possible, this dream will only become a reality when we commit to learning, evaluating, and practising the principles capable of emerging into a thriving marriage.

Challenges are inevitable and will arise even in the most beautiful marriage. It is not the presence of difficulties that destroys a union, but our response. A series of difficult situations does not mean that the union was not ordained; rather, it highlights the need for urgent action, pointing you back to the vow you made at the initiation of the marriage.

About two months into our marriage, Danielle and I had a trivial disagreement, and I stormed out of the house into my car and drove back to work. This response had become a recurring scene in our marriage. At the time, I thought the best way to resolve and prevent conflicts from escalating was to leave. I believed our temporary separation would ultimately bring peace and somehow preserve the marriage. However, sometimes the easiest thing to do is not the best. Avoiding the situation and declining to talk was futile. Avoid stonewalling, invest in conversation, listen to each other, and choose the best path for the union. "Running away, avoiding life's battles, or giving up robs you of the opportunity to grow and be stronger." — Innocent Mwatsikesimbe

Not expecting to see me in camp, my squad corporal called out as I tried to pass the guard's room quietly and unnoticed, "What are you doing here, pastor?" I replied, "I cannot bother with the woman at my house. She is too miserable. It is better if I stay here in camp." "Did you drive back here all the way from St Mary?" he asked. "Yes," I responded, "that is actually easy." He continued, "Pastor, I know you are an adult, and I can't tell you what to do, but I can't help but notice the speed at which you entered the camp. Is this how you drove from St Mary?" I explained, "Yes, Corporal, I was upset, and it makes me feel better."

"Pastor, I am not perfect, and I made a lot of mistakes that cost me my marriage. You don't have to make those same mistakes if you listen and learn from me. It is an attitude like that motivated my wife to walk away and divorce me. You can't keep running from the problem. I realised that our society and its norms have marred us as men and emboldened us to behave like tyrants, but we must undo such socialisation and culture in our minds. Pastor do not allow what happened to me to happen to you," he lamented. "How do you think your wife would feel if you had an accident on your way here today? Do you remember Becky?" he asked. I remembered Becky well. He was a promising Lance corporal who recently lost his life in a car accident because he, too, was trying to evade disagreement with his spouse. At that moment, the tears began to flow. As I reflected on everything he said, I knew I needed to improve how I communicated. If my marriage was to thrive, I had to desist from stonewalling.

What is Stonewalling?

Stonewalling is behaviour intended to delay or obstruct by refusing to answer questions or being evasive. According to John Gottman it is a situation in which one partner withdraws from the conversation and stops engaging. He further postulates that it may be expressed as:

- turning around and looking away or displaying disinterest in what is being discussed.
- the silent treatment
- physically leaving the room
- refusing to answer or discuss the issue.
- shouting to end the conversation.

Listening to my squad corporal that day made me realise the extent to which our social upbringing can affect how we make decisions, resolve conflicts, and manage expectations. No one comes to a marriage empty; we all come with varying attachments, including our views, cultural norms, expectations, behaviours, and experiences which can either inspire or hamper the union's progress. Everyone has an unconscious tendency to reflect on their environment. Studies show that individuals who grow up in positive family climates with effective parenting are more likely to have healthy romantic relationships. Additionally, persons who are more assertive and behave positively with their families also help create a positive marriage and family climate. Several are affected today because of the impact of past experiences of their spouse. Carefully assess your daily happenings to see to what extent you are affected. Becoming aware is the first step to rescuing yourself and ultimately saving the marriage.

Growing up, my father would always leave the house when there was a disagreement. In our home, "walking away" was totally tolerable. Subconsciously, I became what I was taught. On the contrary, Danielle would always try to resolve conflicts quickly, as this was the practice in her home. Differences in upbringing can affect how we settle disputes in the union. It is therefore imperative that one undergoes a thorough reflection to recognise the varying social norms, experiences, and qualities you are onboarding into the marriage. Honesty and transparency are essential to the health and longevity of the union. Commence the journey to a thriving marriage by becoming more aware of your personality, needs, and shortcomings. Becoming more in tune with self will build strength and character to honour God and provide excellent service to your spouse.

"Pastor, I am not putting you back on duty, go home; whatever it is, God can help you to resolve it," Corporal James proclaimed. With tears in my eyes, I thanked him for the insight, shook his hand, picked up my belongings, and headed to the car". From the gate, he shouted, "Go get some of that fluff. Give your wife a night she will never forget". Jokingly, I stood at attention, saluted, and shouted yes, sir. Corporal James was so accommodating. He redirected my focus and showed me the importance of working on my marriage. That evening, I drove home, and surprisingly, my incredible wife could not wait to get a hold of me. I felt and experienced intimacy in a new dimension. Her touch and soft voice sent chills all over my body. The ambiance was right, and the mood was great. "Thinking of you keeps me awake. Dreaming of you keeps me asleep. Being with you keeps me alive." — Unknown.

That was a welcome worth remembering. I was driven to speak, and my wife accommodated my thoughts and feelings. Stonewalling often occurs when we become overwhelmed, losing our ability to focus. It is then that we try to escape, forgetting that we are a team fighting for the same cause. Your spouse is not your opponent; you are both working to have a thriving marriage. Suppressing our true thoughts, feelings, and ideas may deter explosion, but deep down, we implode, often leading to poor decisions that could have lifelong consequences, even health and mental issues. As you work to contain the explosion, you relieve yourself of the inner burden. Speak openly and honestly while showing regard and empathy for your spouse.

Though defensiveness, anger, contempt, and criticism are common with individuals, men are more likely to stonewall. Husbands do not give power to your ego; give your energy to finding a resolution. Researchers believe women are naturally more soothing because of their biological makeup, as they produce more oxytocin, a hormone that helps with relaxation. Being aware of this can be advantageous for the couple, as wives can work to create a relationship-friendly environment that encourages conversation. Turn the lights off, set up a nice date in the open, wear something sexy, and use your body to soothe your partner to peace skilfully. Men tend to perceive life as having only two options in disagreement: fight or flight. Genks, there is a third option called "Let's talk!" Pop champagne, start your favourite role-play, spank her on the ass, stare her deep in the eyes, and give her all of you, including your full attention. Pull her close and reassure her that she is where you belong and is the queen of your heart. Stonewalling is a sign that your partner is losing hope and is becoming discouraged. Do everything in your power to restore that trust and remind your spouse of their worth. A gentle hug, remaining still, and whispering the most sexy and appealing thing can help create an atmosphere conducive to talking. Stonewalling has detrimental effects on both men and women alike. When men stonewall, it has the propensity to hurt women. Levenson and Gottman (1985) opines that women's heart rate jumps when men stonewall. Brothers, our duty is to serve our spouses, not destroy them. Try to resolve conflicts quickly, discuss matters urgently and in good time, and top it off with some spontaneous sexual adventure. Stonewalling only slowly destroys the union by:

- escalating and prolonging arguments,
- leaves problems unresolved,
- create emotional disconnection,
- triggers hopelessness.

Over the years, Danielle and I have developed ways to communicate even in the most difficult times. Sometimes, this is through writing; however, I have committed to never leaving my home again. We do not need to fight or flight; we can talk. One of the most important roles of a spouse, husband, or wife, is to lift each other, especially when things are complicated. We all have hard times and days in which nothing seems to go right. Invest in your spouse today for a brighter and more productive future together.

Dear couple,

In marriage, overcoming stonewalling is akin to dismantling barriers and fostering an environment of open communication and understanding. Stonewalling, a silent but potent hurdle, obstructs the flow of connection and resolution within relationships. Overcoming it requires patience, empathy, and a commitment to breaking down walls rather than building them higher. It involves a conscious effort to replace withdrawal and silence with active engagement and a willingness to listen and understand, even amidst disagreement. Couples navigate this challenge by creating a safe space where both partners feel comfortable expressing their thoughts and emotions without fear of judgment. Overcoming stonewalling in marriage demands a shared dedication to nurturing dialogue and empathy, laying the foundation for deeper understanding, healing, and a stronger bond between partners.

Reflect Now That You Have Proceeded…

Circle the flag light that best describes your assessment of yourself/ partner based on the topic: **Marriage and Stonewalling.**

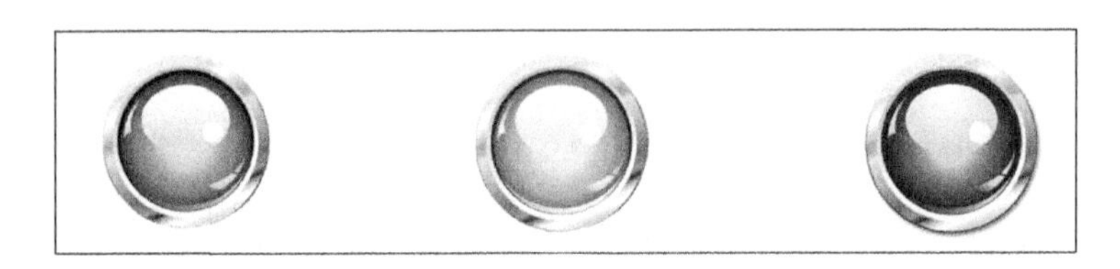

Explain your answer based your previous selection:

Know-Metre: Now appraise your knowledge of this topic after reading by circling the gauge.

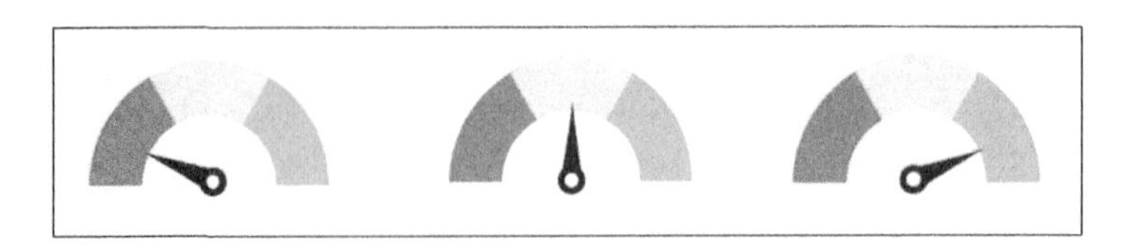

MARRIAGE AND THE MIRROR

Reflections in Marriage: Exploring the Mirror Effect of Self-Discovery, Personal Empowerment and Growth in Relationships.

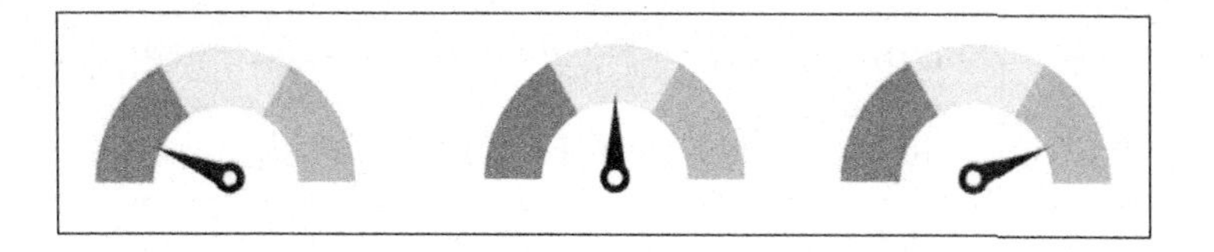

"The best way to find yourself is to lose yourself in the service of others." — Mahatma Gandhi

"Hun, can't you refill the water and put it in the refrigerator when you use it, please?" I called out with immense frustration and annoyance. A repentant Danielle responded, "OK." Still annoyed, I continued, "Every time I have to come to refill the empty container." An even more annoyed Danielle replied, "Do you know the number of things I have to redo that you undo?" "So, this is now a blame game? I am simply asking you to refill the water." I argued. "Nick, do you even consider all I do for this family?" she quizzed. Feeling as though my wife was simply making an excuse, I retreated with no intent of mentioning the same again. Deflection often leads to more arguments and creates a toxic environment. Rather than diverting the blame, listen with empathy, express regret, and commit to improve. Peaceful resolution must be the end goal of every disagreement. It can be difficult to resolve conflicts in relationships. Still, the success of the union relies solely on one's willingness to reflect, acknowledge, admit, apologise, and take action to encourage ongoing peace. You are responsible for your behaviour; only you can change your conduct. Never avoid the problem in the hope of an automatic resolution, as the residue will show up sometime in the future. Here are some steps to consider if you or your spouse struggle with blaming each other:

- **Be empathetic**

Put yourself in your spouse's shoes. Can you see why they might be upset or disappointed? On the other hand, no one wants to be wrongfully blamed for something. How else could you have addressed the problem? Be sensitive to your spouse's needs. External struggles can affect the way they communicate or address issues.

- **Communicate regularly and honestly**

Is there a reason for your spouse's supposing action? Did he or she simply forget? Are they struggling with some other problems? The best way to approach your spouse is to ask. For example, "Did you remove the cup from the table?" Use the sandwich approach to share your disappointment. Start with something positive, share what you intended with compassion, and end with something positive. For instance, "Danielle, you are so hot, I would enjoy making love to you now. Did you remove the container from the refrigerator earlier today? … Alright dear, remember to refill next time. I love you. I can't wait to have you all for myself tonight." Likewise, show concern for your spouse's feelings if you are the person in error. For example: "Oh, honey, I am so sorry. I will try not to let this happen again." Conversation is the best route to avoid escalating an argument; use it wisely. Remember, your response is supposed to help your partner.

It is not so much what you say but how you say it. Don't only say the right things; manage how you communicate it.

- **Listen to your partner**

As you converse with your partner, be sure to listen to them keenly. Your partner's feelings are as important as yours. Listen to gain insight, collectively decide on what needs to change, and take steps to make the necessary changes progressively. The more you listen to each other, the more likely you are to make wise and constructive decisions. Don't listen merely to respond; instead, listen to understand.

- **Focus on those things you can change**

In the interim, change the things you can change and work on those that require time and resources. What is paramount is that you recognise the need for change and are willing to make progress. Consider the most feasible way for your spouse to share in the process of change. Change is inevitable; people evolve, and so do our needs. Keep learning and amend present shortcomings for a happier tomorrow.

- **Discuss your roles**

As with Danielle and I, most times one partner blames the other because there is a subconscious expectation that one person is responsible for doing something. Your partner is everything except a psychic. Even as observant as he or she is, they may struggle to determine what you need. Always communicate expectations clearly. For instance, maybe Danielle was unaware that I expected her to refill the container and return it to the refrigerator after use. Not everything is universal; some things are just personal expectations. Share them lovingly.

- **Know when to let things go**

You cannot argue about everything. At some point you must choose peace over rightness. Communicate clearly and honestly, let go of grudges and malice, and forgive quickly.

- **Be gracious**

Be quick to show kindness and compassion to your spouse. At some point, we will all need grace and empathy. Always extend the same grace you would if the roles were reversed.

Sometimes, our demands can outweigh our appreciation for each other. Similarly, regular deflection can override our need to empathise. Always remember that you are a team. The team either succeeds or fails. Support each other constantly and bear each other's burdens. "Love and compassion are necessities, not luxuries. Without them, a marriage cannot survive." —Dalai Lama

A moment of weakness should attract our attention and stimulate our passion and commitment to each other. Getting married does not mean the end of personal failure; your failures become clearer through proximal interaction. No one knows your flaws better than your spouse; trust their assessment and commit to a path of growth. The thing that makes you miserable is a signpost to develop empathy. Your spouse is the mirror through which you will better discover yourself. Respond positively to feedback and be gracious to each other when you comment on the noticeable inadequacies. While we empathize, undesired practices are not to be ignored. In the first century, Paul acknowledged that individuals would fail; however, when they did, it was the responsibility of their partners to aid in the restorative process.

Live creatively, friends. If someone falls into sin, forgivingly restore him, saving your critical comments for yourself. You might be needing forgiveness before the day's out. Stoop down and reach out to those who are oppressed. Share their burdens, and so complete Christ's law. If you think you are too good for that, you are badly deceived. — Galatians 6:1-3

The overtaken spouse needs to be restored. He or she should not be ignored, and neither should they be excused. Please do not destroy or humiliate them. Doing so is a platform to highlight how perfect you are and how flawed he or she is. The wise partner always seeks restoration.

After careful reflection, I recognised how selfish and inconsiderate I was, complaining about a container that needed to be refilled, something that would have taken me less than two minutes to do. Selfishness is among the leading threats to harmony in a marriage. The moment it becomes about your rightness is the instant that you fail to consider your spouse's needs, relinquishing an opportunity to serve. Marriage is the joining of two imperfect people committing to support each other, graciously recognising each other's weaknesses, and simultaneously helping your partner patiently. Selfishness is the mark of immaturity and deters bonding, stirring up strife and forming a platform to criticise rather than to help your spouse. Our selfish attitude leads to resentment and poor communication, stifles happiness in the home, destroys trust and loyalty, and disregards your spouse's well-being. In essence, a selfish partner does more to destroy the marriage than to help the marriage thrive. A selfish/narcissistic partner thinks more about self and what will make them happy, but a considerate spouse considers their spouse and how they can help. When the attitude we pursue is the latter, we will always take steps to support rather than complain or criticise.

This situation brought to the forefront the state of my heart: selfish and self-made perfectionist, with little empathy for others, even my own wife. My insensitivity to my wife's shortcomings revealed my own imperfections, the things I needed to improve to become more civil, loving, and caring.

Reflect today! Ask yourself:

1. What am I learning about myself from the things that deeply annoy and frustrate me?
2. What lessons can I learn from my partner's presumed failure?

Write your thoughts in the space below:

Self-reflection is an opportunity to grow and understand who you are, what you value, and how you think. When you know your true self and future needs, you can serve your spouse empathetically. This process will help strengthen your relationship and embolden you to share with your partner the things that bother you honestly. At times, you may need to apologize for your behaviour. This is instrumental in preventing the same behaviour in the future. At that moment, I apologized sincerely to my wife and vowed to take action to avoid a reprisal.

Frequent self-evaluation will highlight areas for improvement. It also helps you understand your current relationship even better, resulting in you appreciating your partner. Self-reflection allows us to take a hard look at who we are and how we can be better.

Dear couple,
Remember, your relationship starts with you. When you are becoming your best self, you will attract true and long-lasting love. The power to create the love relationship that you desire is in your hands.

Reflect Now That You Have Proceeded...

Circle the flag light that best describes your assessment of yourself/ partner based on the topic: **Marriage and the Mirror.**

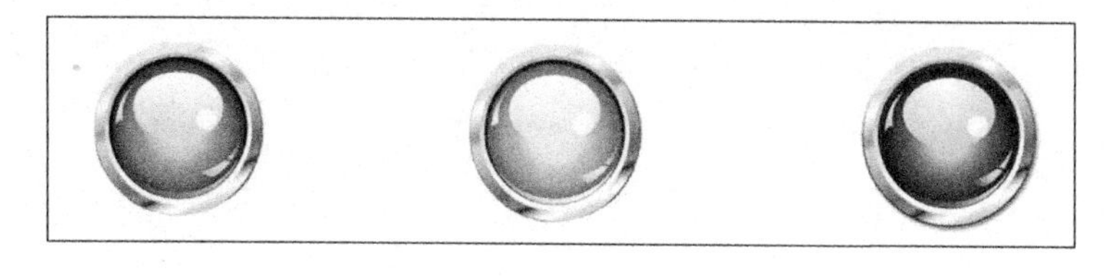

Explain your answer based your previous selection:

Know-Metre: Now appraise your knowledge of this topic after reading by circling the gauge.

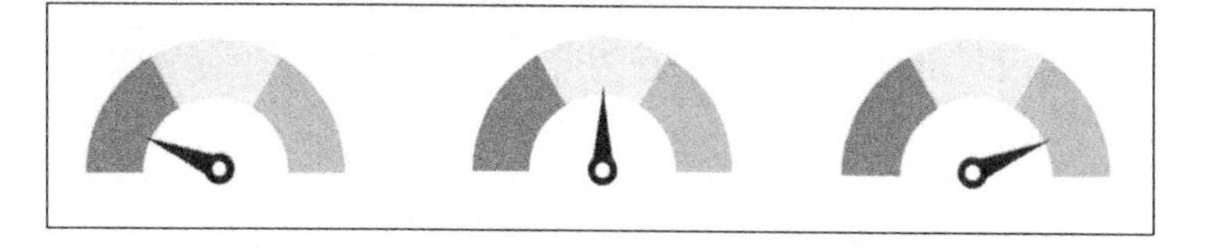

MARRIAGE AND GRATTITUDE

Celebrating Love: The Power of Mutual Appreciation in Sustaining a Fulfilling Marriage

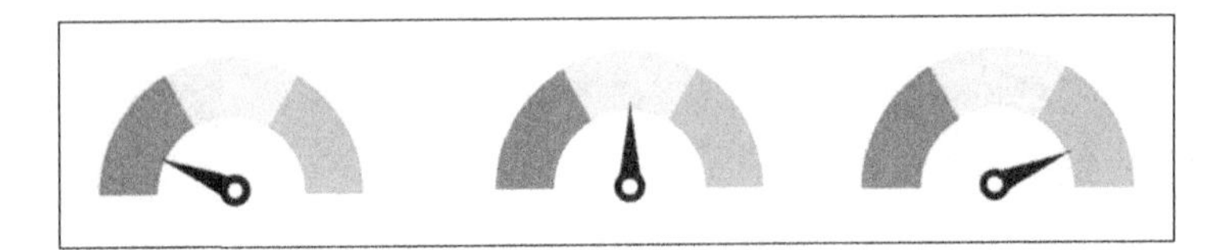

"Marriage, ultimately, is the practice of becoming passionate friends."
—Harville Hendrix

After about four years of marriage, we asked my dad how important it is to show appreciation in marriage. As the usual humorous storyteller, he decided to illustrate the importance through a story. He told us of a couple living in Westmoreland, the westmost parish on the island of Jamaica. They had recently married, and the wife was now studying in Kingston, at least five (5) to six (6) hours away. As such, she opted to board at a facility there to allow an easier commute to school. This meant that the couple would often not see each other until midsemester. At the time, the couple needed to be better off enough to afford a vehicle, and public transportation was not as regular and prevalent as today.

Furthermore, the husband had to work in Westmoreland to help support her in school. Clearly, one would understand why the couple would find it almost impossible to see each other. To further their dismay, the only access to phones was the "blue box" public phone, and you had to wait long periods to access the service. With the couple's tight and differing schedules, this was hard; therefore, their mode of communication was by letter writing. The wife's birthday was fast approaching, and the husband thought about how he could show my appreciation to his wife. Despite their difficult situations, she remained faithful, caring, loving, and understanding. He thought long and hard about what to do; then, he remembered the mango tree in the centre of the yard. It had just started to bear, and because he knew she loved mangoes, he thought sending the first fruit from the tree to her in Kingston would be good. He rushed out of the house with a box and grabbed his picking stick. Much to his amazement, he found three lovely mangoes, and he decided to name them love, commitment, and care, the things he appreciated most about his wife. He cleaned the mangoes, wrapped them in newspaper and packaged them in a box, rushed to the post office, and mailed the package with a note: "Because I appreciate you". He eagerly awaited his wife's return note confirming she had received the package. After two weeks, he still hadn't received a reply, so he waited some more. Unfortunately, the Post office workers' union could not secure a deal with the government, so members decided to take industrial action for a week. This meant that all packages, including the three mangoes, were stuck in transit. After about a week, the workers had some settlement, so work resumed at the post. The package arrived three weeks later than the expected date. The wife, who had not heard from her husband for a whole month, rushed to the post office to see if he had sent a letter. As she anticipated, he did send an entire package for her. At home, she opened the box to find the remains of three spoilt mangoes with the note, "Because I appreciate you". She began to cry. The mangoes were spoilt, but the words were profound. She penned, "When I received the mangoes, they were spoilt, but it's not the gift that counts, it's the thought. Thank you, hun, and I appreciate you!". After a week, the long-anticipated response arrived at the post. The husband eagerly picked up the note, read it, and cried. He was disappointed that the mangoes didn't go as expected but was moved that his wife saw the value in his effort.

Appreciation is crucial to a thriving marriage; everyone wants to feel valued. We want to know that our spouses are actively thinking about us and equally appreciate the things we do. Therefore, appreciation is the ability to recognise and celebrate our spouses for the qualities they possess and for the kindness and selflessness through which they exhibit care and concern toward us. Though exchanging gifts is vital, appreciation is not limited to giving them; it is first the recognition of one's worth and an expression of sincere gratitude. Appreciation is, therefore, one of the most essential love languages for growing intimacy in a relationship. Psychologists using the magic dot ratio to weigh positive and negative interactions in marriage have suggested that for every negative exchange, there is the need for five positive interactions to compensate or make amends. If we aren't careful, we will spend more time focussing on the negative rather than the positive. Mrs. James's reaction to the spoilt mangoes in the story was quite exemplary. There must have been the temptation to ask why he packaged mangoes all the way from Westmoreland, knowing well that there was a high probability that it would not have arrived on time. She could also reason that the mangoes were spoiled; hence, there was nothing to be grateful for. Instead, she looked beyond the spoils and recognised the thought and effort of her husband. Sometimes people don't want more gifts. They just want to be valued. Mr James clearly valued his wife. Without even considering the likelihood of them spoiling, he thought about showing her how much he appreciated her love, care, and faithfulness.

Reflection: What do you appreciate about your spouse?

Dear spouse,

After you say I do, you must continue to show your partner appreciation. This helps to keep the lines of communication open while allowing you to feel good about your spouse. A happy partner amounts to a happy and fulfilled marital experience. Appreciation is one of the most important ways to demonstrate love. Consequently, love isn't only a noun but a verb. It is to be demonstrated. Don't only verbalize love; show it through your actions. Today, think of ways to show your spouse appreciation and remind them of your unwavering love. Below are a few ways to consider:

- words of affirmation,
- acts of service,
- sharing gifts,
- spending quality time with them,
- physical interaction (hugs, kisses, touching, holding hands,
- taking them dates,
- writing and sharing letters expressing your appreciation,
- leaving them a card,
- sharing in activities that your spouse enjoys,
- giving them your full attention while listening to them,
- support and encourage their dreams.

True appreciation affects our behaviour and how we treat and interact with each other. When we appreciate our spouse, we:

- listen more,
- forgive quickly,
- are more patient,
- show more empathy,
- show kindness,
- give them grace,
- enjoy their company,
- serve them excellently.

Reflection: To what extent do you appreciate your spouse?

Rating Scale

Extremely	☐
Mostly	☐
Somewhat	☐
Maybe	☐

Explain your answer.

To what extent do you feel appreciated?

Rating Scale	
Extremely	☐
Mostly	☐
Somewhat	☐
Maybe	☐

Explain your answer.

When we fail to recognise our partners and their worth, indirectly, we insinuate that they are worthless and unappreciated. Prioritise consistently expressing kindness through both words and actions. "Kind words are like honey — sweet to the soul and healthy for the body" —Proverbs 16:24 (NLT).

Kindness and appreciation strengthen our bond and rekindle our love for each other. As we reflected on the powerful lesson taught by Mr. Brown, we promised each other to always recognise the sacrifices and contributions we make in the union. The results have been remarkable; we have grown closer and are unafraid to declare our passionate love for each other.

Dear couple,
Celebrate your spouse and build a stronger marriage. Like Mr and Mrs James, it is not the gifts but the thought that counts. You do not need a lot of money, nor do you need to wait until you get a vacation. Start now, recognise your spouse's sacrifice, and express your kindness to them. Expressing gratitude, big or small, builds respect and trust in relationships. Do not withhold appreciation any longer.

Reflect Now That You Have Proceeded...

Circle the flag light that best describes your assessment of yourself/ partner based on the topic: **Marriage and Self Care.**

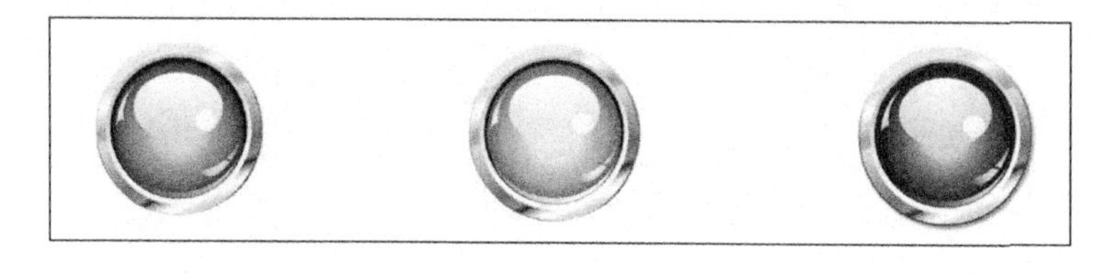

Explain your answer based your previous selection:

Know-Metre: Now appraise your knowledge of this topic after reading by circling the gauge.

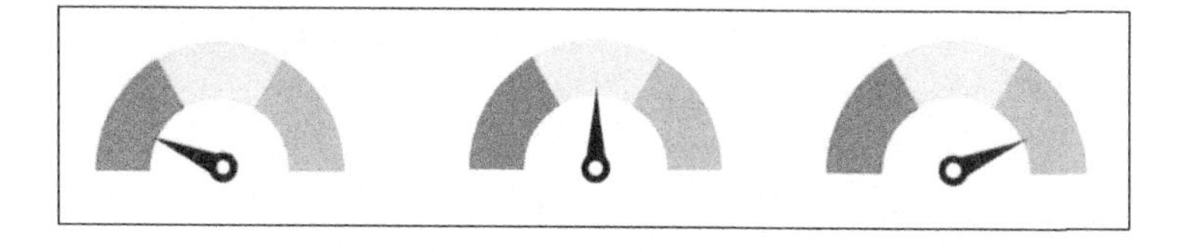

MARRIAGE AND SELF CARE

Balancing Love and Self-Care: Nurturing Individual-being within the Framework of Marriage.

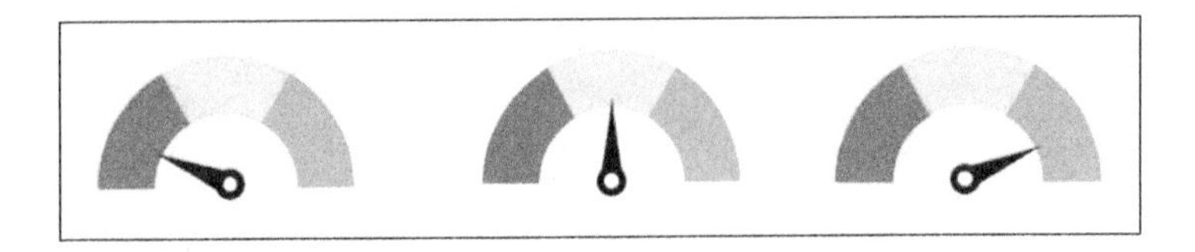

"Almost everything will work again if you unplug it a few minutes, including you." — Unknown

Make time for self-care. Our family relocated to the United Kingdom, far from home and relatives. Soon after settling, we found ourselves in lockdown due to the global Covid-19 pandemic. This brought various disruptions, including school closures, and we were forced into home confinement. With my background as a trained teacher and the uncertainties ahead, we decided to homeschool our five and three-year-old children. Initially, my husband had to work from home, adjusting to a new teaching job and the challenges of the education system, causing significant stress.

In the midst of caring for my family, supporting my husband's ministry, and taking complete charge of my children's education, I found myself constantly occupied. I assumed a packed schedule, rising early and often being the last to rest, neglecting my own need for rest and relaxation. Despite encouragement from friends and ministry partners, I continued to push myself without considering self-care.The ongoing lockdown further compounded our situation, limiting our ability to go outside or even take a simple walk. Driven by my dedication to my roles as wife, mother, friend, and minister, I neglected my personal needs. It's easy to get so caught up in life's demands that we overlook the significance of personal time.

Refrain from being engrossed in activities that you neglect: rest, healthy eating, and time for yourself. Just like any machine that requires regular servicing and refuelling, we, as individuals, also need maintenance and rejuvenation. A car needs routine maintenance and fuel from a gas station, while a computer requires a reboot to restore its components and enhance its performance. If these devices are not serviced, they will become less effective and eventually non-functional. Similarly, people need self-care to function at their best. It is, therefore, crucial to take steps to preserve and improve your health to be effective in your role as a spouse.

One morning, I got up heartily and started my routine, but soon after, I began to feel ill. This was unlike me; I knew something was wrong but couldn't pinpoint it. I called my mom and tried to explain how I felt. She encouraged me to take a break, so I decided to listen and quickly retreated to my bedroom. My husband came in and realized I was unwell, and being sensitive to my need for space took on the rest of the chores and supervision of the children for the afternoon. He prepared dinner and later checked in to see how I was doing. Being overwhelmed, I didn't even respond to him. Thankfully, he is observant and usually discerns accurately; at that moment, he knew I needed some time alone. He ensured that the children did not disturb me for the rest of the evening. That night, I got some rest and woke up feeling better, so I decided to go for a walk. On the walk, I reflected on the events that had transpired during the past week. I recall having several mood swings, which led to arguments and made me unusually uneasy—the time alone really helped me to reset and become revived. I felt more energised and became much more patient and understanding. I was now able to serve my family and online community better. Marriage requires much work, but do not ignore the importance of personal time and self-care. It is through self-care that we become well enough to perform our duties efficiently and effectively. With proper self-care, we can function at a higher standard under stressful circumstances. The World Health Organisation defines self-care as "the ability of individuals, families, and communities to promote health, prevent disease, maintain health, and to cope with illness and disability with or without the support of a healthcare provider." Therefore, self-care is not limited to rest and revival but includes everything we do to remain physically healthy. This entails hygiene, nutrition, and seeking medical care when needed. It is all the steps an individual indulges in to manage stressors in life and take care of their health and well-being. Self-care requires regularly checking in with ourselves, asking how we are doing and what our body needs.

Dear spouse,

This is a wellness check. Now that you have said I do, how are you doing?

What is your body desirous of?

Choose from this self-care list and add more where needed.

- Sleep ☐
- Rest ☐
- Alone time ☐
- Food ☐
- Exercise ☐
- Meditation ☐
- Prayer ☐
- Others: ____________________

Remember, self-care is unique to each person and may change from day to day. What one person requires may differ from what you need, and what you need today may change tomorrow. Therefore, paying keen attention to your body and what it requires is essential. Self-care should be intentional, deliberate, and regular.

Dear couple,

Although you can't always predict when your body will require special attention, you can set aside time weekly for self-care and reflection. This will deter you from becoming overwhelmed and help you put your best foot forward.

Task: In the timetable provided, enter a time slot that is solely dedicated to self-care. Communicate this to your spouse and household members so that they can support you on this journey to continuous wholeness.

	Physical	*Emotional*	*Spiritual*
MON			
TUES			
WED			
THURS			
FRI			

Good self-care results in positive health outcomes such as a reduction in stress, an improved immune system, increased productivity, and higher self-esteem. Self-care is emotional, physical, and spiritual; hence, ensure you are catering to all three:

Emotional Self-care entails but is not limited to: -

- self-talk and words of affirmation
- weekly activities you enjoy, such as having a bubble bath, spa date, or watching a movie.
- saying "no" to things or requests that can cause unwanted stress.
- taking regular breaks

Physical Self-care: -

- ensure you prioritise sleep and rest.
- engage in daily or weekly personal exercise or join a gym.
- eat well-balanced and healthy meals.

Spiritual Self-care: -

- join a church community or upliftment group.
- pray and meditate frequently.
- maintain a gratitude journal.

Dear couple,

Devise a self-care plan for effective implementation. To do this :

- determine what activities you enjoy or those necessary for refuelling your energy while being attainable given your schedule.
- start simple. choose one activity that you can easily fit into your schedule.
- turn your phones off or put away anything else that may disrupt the process.
- reflect, evaluate, change, or continue if necessary.
- add additional activities as necessary.
- get support from your spouse, friends, or other accessible person.
- journal, capture, record, and reflect on the progress.
- discuss your progress with someone.
- enjoy the process.

Self-care is putting a pause on everything else while zooming in on ourselves and asking what satisfies us. Dear spouse, reflect passionately today on the ensuing task. Follow the tips above to start a successful self-care program. Encourage your partner to take a similar journey. Remember, we serve each other better when revived, empowered, and rejuvenated. Start the process today.

What brings you satisfaction?

When will be your first day of implementation?

Marriage and self-care intertwine like threads in a tapestry, forming the foundation for a resilient and fulfilling relationship. Self-care within marriage isn't selfish; instead, it's an act of love and preservation, nurturing one's well-being to better contribute to the partnership. It involves recognising personal needs, boundaries, and passions while honouring the individuality of each partner. By prioritising self-care, individuals within a marriage cultivate a healthier mindset, which enriches the relationship. It's about finding balance, where personal growth and fulfilment complement the shared journey as a couple. When both partners prioritise their well-being, they bring their best selves to the union, fostering an environment of mutual support and understanding and enriching the marriage with vitality and resilience.

Reflect Now That You Have Proceeded...

Circle the flag light that best describes your assessment of yourself/ partner based on the topic: **Marriage and Self Care.**

Explain your answer based your previous selection:

Know-Metre: Now appraise your knowledge of this topic after reading by circling the gauge.

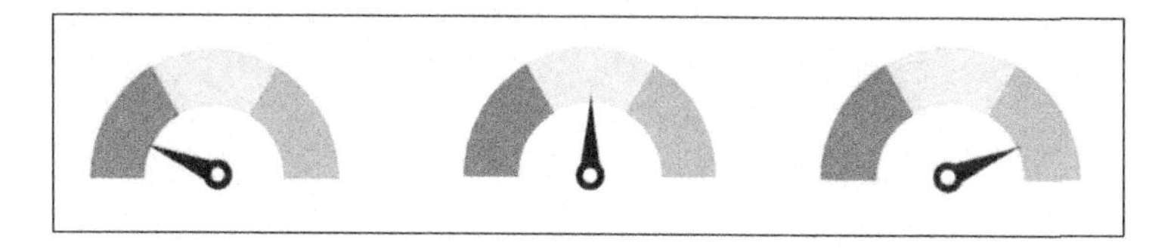

MARRIAGE AND PARENTING

Journey Together: Navigating the Challenges and Joys of marriage and Parenting.

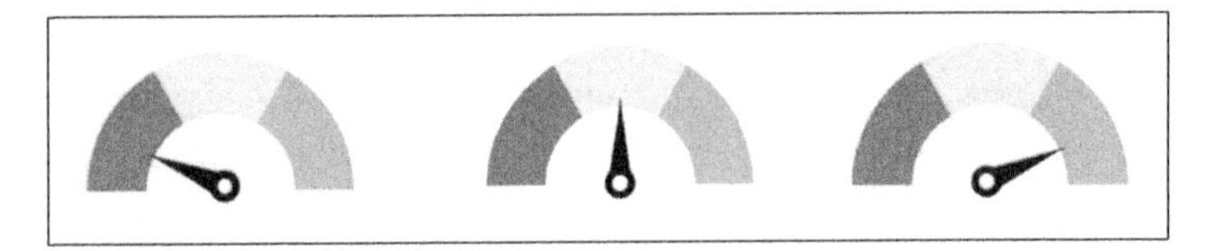

"Parenting has nothing to do with perfection. Perfection isn't even the goal, not for us, not for our children. Learning together to live well in an imperfect world, loving each other despite or even because of our imperfections, and growing as humans while we grow our little humans, those are the goals of gentle parenting. So don't ask yourself at the end of the day if you did everything right. Ask yourself what you learned and how well you loved, then grow from your answer. That is perfect parenting." — L.R. Knost

What is parenting?

Parenting is the process of raising children and providing them with protection and care to ensure their healthy development into adulthood. Parents are the longest-serving teachers and are best placed to influence their children's development. Therefore, as influencers, the parents must ensure that the child learns, grows, and matures into a responsible adult. Effective parenting requires investing considerable time into raising and developing the child. Our duty as parents should be equally important as our commitment as a couple to each other. Please do not neglect this call, as it can be detrimental to your child's health, security, and development. Every day, parents make choices and act deliberately to help shape their children into people with character, respect, a sense of responsibility, motivation, and skills to help them succeed as kids and adults. Take the time to bond with your children in a meaningful and productive manner. The parent's effectiveness is not measured merely by how the child is treated and how they conduct themselves as a child but by the kind of adult they become.

Parenting is difficult

Some years ago, I took on the monumental task of constructing a perimeter wall along with two massive concrete posts at the entrance of our property to provide security. Just the thought of constructing this wall felt complicated and overwhelming, given that I had no experience in construction. Still, I was determined to do what was necessary to ensure the safety and security of my family. Similarly, parenting can feel like an enormous and demanding task, especially when we are aspiring parents. However, with two loving, committed individuals joining together in marriage, we can impact and shape our children's lives. Despite having no skill in building construction, I was committed to learn. Likewise, parenting does not have to be something you try to figure out on your own along the way; employ the necessary resources to support your practice and deliver meaningful resources. Become a catalyst of change, always desiring a better experience for those you lead (your children).

Attitude of the successful parent

Parents can succeed in parenting if they develop the attitude and passion to pursue the outcome envisioned in their children. Successful parents:

- **understands their roles and excels at them.** Our approach to parenting must mimic how God treats and develops us. In the very same way he loves, guides, protects, cares, provides, encourages, communicates, listens, disciplines, and leads us, we must support our children. God's handling of humanity must be the template for human development.

- **are not perfect.** However, they are action-driven and purposeful. Therefore, they will take the necessary steps to ensure their children grow, develop, and mature into successful human beings. The act of parenting is an art and should not be perceived as a science; thus, successful parents learn, adjust, adopt, and enjoy their role as parents. They are compassionate and understanding towards their children. They do not have unrealistic expectations of their children and perceive themselves as supporters of their children's progress.

- **are not timid.** They are unafraid of failure but willing to learn from mistakes, admit when they are wrong, and take the appropriate steps to right past wrongs. Successful parents are reflective teachers who plan and execute tomorrow's goals purposefully.

- **pursue support.** They take advantage of the resources available and are committed to lifelong learning. They build and join communities to support each other, knowing that poor parenting anywhere impacts communities, schools, and nations.

- **strive to be good examples** of what they expect of their children. Parents must be convicted practitioners of what they believe is right and lead by example. They resolve conflicts quickly, apologise when they are wrong, and listen attentively.

- **work as a team.** They discuss and make meaningful plans and decisions. They also value the feelings and emotions of their children.

Dear couple,

You can succeed at parenting when you are passionate about raising worthwhile citizens. Understandably, parenting is hard work, but with the right mindset, a thorough understanding of one's call to parent, and the drive to excel, you can create a successful citizen. We can, therefore, infer that parenting is a great call to action: observe, listen, think, and produce a strategic plan to provide not only food and clothing but also care and safety to your children. Great couples make great parents. A family built on the base of marriage, influenced by the parents' love and commitment, provides the stability needed for children to succeed.

Here are some thoughts:

The attainment of any goal requires the stakeholders to believe in the possibilities, sacrifice selflessly, and commit diligently; parenting is no different. We must plan prayerfully, graciously, passionately, and purposefully to ensure we succeed in marriage and parenthood simultaneously.

Dear couple,

After you say I do, spend some time discussing the following questions as you plan to undertake parenthood:

- how many children will we have?
- where will our children live?
- what are the values that we will impart to our children?
- what names will we give to our children and why?
- how will we support their health and education?
- who will be their godparents, and why?
- when will we start having children?
- how will the children be catered for when we must work?
- how will we spend time together as parents?
- do we want to start a family now?
- are we ready to be totally responsible for all my child's needs?
- will we be able to raise my child in a loving and healthy home?
- can we afford to raise a child right now?
- what kind of support will we receive from our family and friends?

- what would having a baby right now mean for our future?
- how would having a baby right now affect our family or other children?

Although plans can change or evolve, we must begin planning for our child's life (from conception to adulthood) from the outset. Our responsibilities will change over time, but we will always be their parents. Parenting can be fun, exciting, and fulfilling, providing a lifetime opportunity to actively aid in the development of your children. Prepare passionately. The love and bond parents share with their children is the most rewarding of all the experiences. Not only does it join parents to children, but it brings the couple together through frequent planning, discussion, and celebrations, and, as such, can be gratifying. After you say I do, begin to prepare for your children with a desired end in mind. This is applicable whether you are an emerging or returning parent.

Dear couple,

How do see your children in the future?

Whether you are an emerging parent or a seasoned parent, to become effective, we must consider the following:

- praying with and encouraging our children.
- recognise challenges and devise solutions.
- make clear expectations.
- teach and discipline our children.
- motivate our children.
- provide them with regular and meaningful feedback and support to ensure their development.

Many people in our contemporary society perceive parenting as simply providing children with basic needs, such as food, a safe place to sleep, and clothing. However, contrary to this, it is a much more in-depth, costly, and committed relationship that incorporates the child's mental, physical, emotional, and spiritual needs.

Dear couple,

The stability of a family is borne out of effective parenting and a good relationship between spouses. Therefore, you must adequately consider your role, carefully analyse the responsibility, and plan effectively to fulfil this call. Having a biological or adopted child means your responsibility is to nurture, provide, protect, and support them in becoming a worthwhile citizen. Regardless of the circumstances, we must provide care, safety, and support to our children. There is no excuse for neglecting your role as parents. Empower yourselves with the tools and training to serve your roles effectively. Your mandate is to provide excellent service to your children even as you cater to your partner's emotional, physical, sexual, and other needs. Your children deserve a stable home with parents, inclusive of a father and mother; both equipped with the ability to provide, feed, clothe, educate, empower, and discipline. Disciplining your child is your fundamental responsibility, not the school or the society.

Parents, the disciplinarian

The concept of discipline commonly evokes the idea of instructing individuals to adhere to rules or a set of behaviours, employing punishment to address disobedience. Both "discipline" and "disciple" originate from the same root word. Discipline suggests a student acquiring knowledge from a proficient instructor. The instructor, in turn, is perceptive and equipped with the right skills to analyse and enact a sequence of steps for fostering positive behaviour in the learner. Therefore, the parent, as a teacher, disciplines the child. Discipline is not abuse, and neither is it punishment. It is simply the child's (learner) ability to practise the correct behaviour independently because they recognise its importance. A child is therefore considered disciplined when they know the desired behaviour and conduct themselves decently because they desire to be like their parents and become an excellent example to others by doing so.

Dear couple,

Do not surrender the work of parenting to society. Fight for your children. One of the most fulfilling contributions you can make to society is rearing productive citizens. You have been handpicked to parent; do it excellently. Identify role models and draw on their expertise, join a course, get counselling, and whatever you do, ensure that you break the cycle of constant erosion of family values. We can succeed at parenting when we parent like a community. Develop a plan for discipline that is intended to help shape your children into productive citizens.

Every implementation should be thoughtful and have a desired outcome in mind. As you plan, remember disciplining your child is hinged on love and not merely appeasement.

Therefore, consider the following:

- discipline is not an exclusive system of rules, regulations, or punishment, nor an invitation to compliance, obedience, or enforcement.

- it is not rigid, unappealing, or a repetitive, overly familiar theme. for example, telling a child to sit in the corner whenever they do something wrong is useless. it may make the children conform out of fear, but he or she will not learn anything.

- discipline is not something others do to a child; it is something the child does for himself or herself. you can receive instruction or guidance from one or many sources, but the source of discipline is not external. it is internal.

- discipline is not obedience to someone else's standards to avoid punishment. it is learning and applying intentional standards to achieve meaningful objectives.

- discipline is not demanded; instead, it is commanded. therefore, it is a choice the child makes to become disciplined as they learn more about your expectations, promises, and consequences. this provides direction and guidance.

Task: Use the guide below to enact a discipline action plan.

What am I doing?

Why am I doing it?

How are we going to achieve our intended goal?

For your child to be successful at discipline there must be:

- clear and shared focus
- high expectations
- frequent monitoring
- regular evaluations
- meaningful feedback
- a system of accountability

The above are elements of a good disciplinarian, one who wants his or her children to do well. The steps are not carried out to cause harm but to strengthen, guide, direct, and produce worthwhile citizens.

Whoever loves discipline loves knowledge, but he who hates reproof is stupid. – Proverbs 12:1.

Styles of parenting and their impact

Having little or no experience in parenting is no excuse for failing to support your child's development. Research or just ask for help. Begin with knowing the different styles of parenting. There are four basic parenting styles:

- **Authoritative:** In this parenting style, the parents are nurturing, responsive, and supportive, yet set firm limits for their children. They attempt to control children's behaviour by explaining rules, discussing, and reasoning. They listen to a child's viewpoint but don't always accept it. Children raised with this style tend to be friendly, energetic, cheerful, self-reliant, self-controlled, curious, cooperative, and achievement oriented.

- **Authoritarian:** A parent who follows an authoritarian approach sets strict rules for kids and may be very adamant about enforcing them without exception. That is, authoritarian parents tend to set firm expectations for their children and always anticipate these expectations and rules to be followed. These parents tend to be less warm and nurturing than others and may only provide their children with a few options or choices. They may overcontrol their children and offer a rigorous "my way or the highway" parenting style. Punishments may be doled out without explanation based on "bad behaviour" that a child might not fully understand. Children raised in this style of household may have low self-esteem and seem shy or even fearful around other people, perhaps because of the fear they've felt living with authoritarian parents. These children may have difficulty in social settings, difficulty making choices on their own, and tend to conform to those around them. Children of authoritarian parents often associate obedience or even success with love (due to how their strict parents show love). They may feel that they aren't loved if they aren't doing exactly what they are told or have somehow made someone unhappy.

- **Permissive:** In this parenting style, parents are warm but lax. They fail to set firm limits, monitor their children's activities closely, or require appropriately mature behaviour from their children. Children raised with this parenting style tend to be impulsive, rebellious, aimless, domineering, aggressive, and low in self-reliance, self-control, and achievement.

- **Uninvolved/neglecting:** In this parenting style, parents are unresponsive, unavailable, and rejecting. Children raised with this parenting style tend to have low self-esteem and little self-confidence and seek other, sometimes inappropriate, role models to substitute for the neglectful parent.

Parenting may be considered child- or parent-centred and regarded as nurturing or controlling.

When we sacrifice to invest in resources that will aid in our improved parenting skills and enforce the strategies learnt, we will be able to celebrate the accomplishments that will result, knowing we would have done our very best and it has yielded good fruit. No matter how discouraged or overwhelmed you may become on the journey, keep toiling, and you will find satisfaction in your efforts rather than facing the regrets of not giving enough. The danger of ineffective parenting is that children are left at the mercy of life, predators, and childhood inexperience.

Your contribution will begin to chart the change needed for a better community, nation, and economy.

Being cognisant of the tumultuous task ahead in constructing the wall and being aware of the shortage of skills needed to finish the job successfully, I consulted a friend for assistance. Like building a wall, parenting can be difficult, especially for an amateur. However, it is not impossible. Coupled with parenting challenges and a lack of skills necessary to carry out our tasks effectively, we may become overwhelmed.

Marriage and parenting intertwine to form a dynamic partnership, a shared adventure filled with joys, challenges, and boundless love. Parenthood within a marriage is a collaborative endeavour where partners navigate the joys and complexities of raising children together. It's a journey that demands unity, understanding, and a shared vision as couples navigate the responsibilities, decisions, and nurturing of their children. Successful parenting within marriage often thrives on open communication, mutual respect, and a willingness to adapt and grow as a team. It's a delicate balance of supporting each other's parenting styles, providing a stable foundation for children, and cherishing the unique bond that evolves not just between parents and child but between partners as they witness and participate in the wonders of nurturing and guiding a new generation.

Task: Use the diagram below to determine what kind of parent you are:

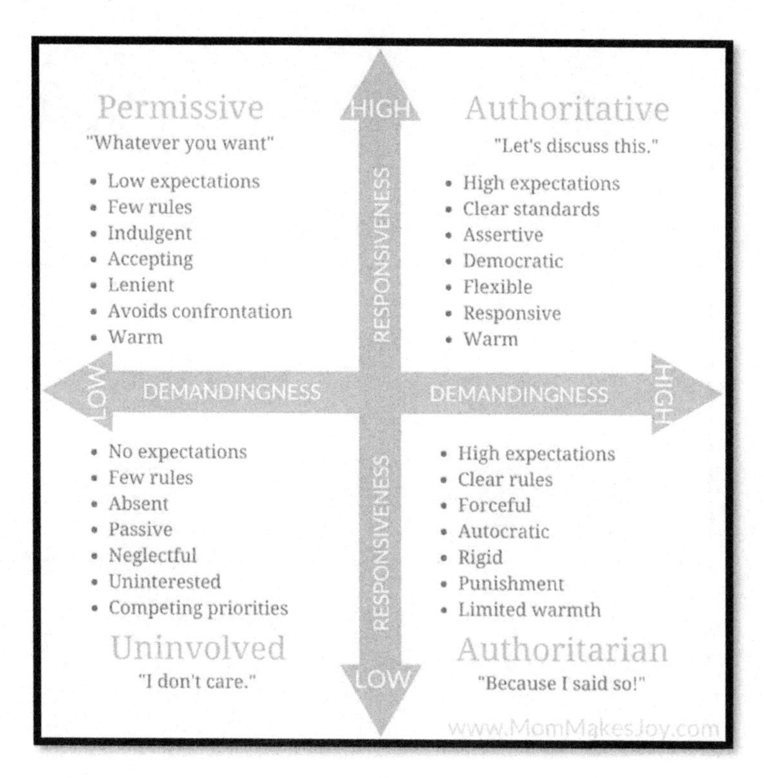

Reflect Now That You Have Proceeded...

Circle the flag light that best describes your assessment of yourself/ partner based on the topic: **Marriage and Parenting.**

Explain your answer based your previous selection:

Know-Metre: Now appraise your knowledge of this topic after reading by circling the gauge.

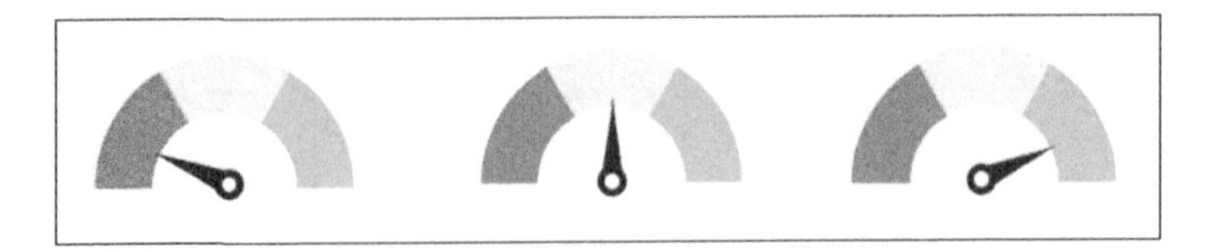

MARRIAGE, FORGIVENESS AND RECONCILIATION

Healing Bonds: The Role of Forgiveness and Reconciliation in Strengthening Marital Relationships.

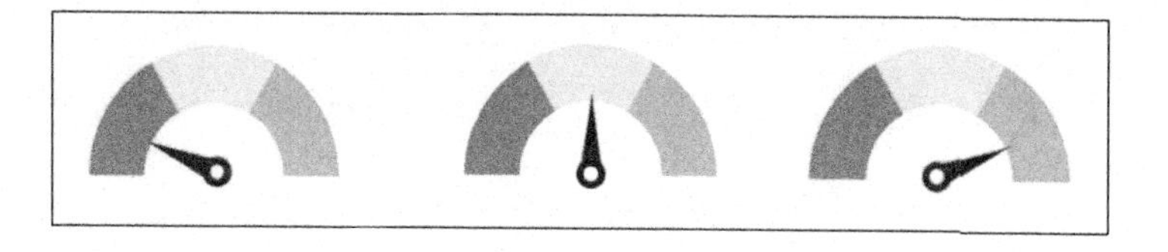

"A happy marriage is a union of two good forgivers."

—Robert Quillen

Within marriage, couples are likely to experience challenges that often result in dissent, which can fracture the relationship. Therefore, the ability to forgive, admit error, take responsibility for an action done, and seek forgiveness is one of the most significant factors that enables the longevity of the relationship. Interpersonal offenses and conflicts can significantly impact couples, causing emotional distress and strain on their mental and physical health. Such emotional distress can have adverse effects on our mental health, leading to stress, anxiety, or depression. It can also manifest physically, impacting our immune system, causing fatigue, and affecting our overall health. How we handle and recover from these challenging experiences is vital to our happiness and well-being. While marriage is not solely for happiness, life without happiness is painful. Conflicts not resolved can lead to feelings of betrayal, hurt, anger, or mistrust. The consequences of unresolved conflicts can lead to a tumultuous marriage; thus, recovery is necessary. Recovery from these experiences often involves forgiveness and communication. How we respond and manage the aftermath of these incidents is pivotal.

Resilience, empathy, and the ability to forgive and move forward contribute significantly to our emotional healing and the restoration of relationships. Forgiveness is often difficult and accompanied by shame and embarrassment. Seeking support from friends, family, or professional help can aid in the healing process. Strategies such as counselling, mediation, or therapy can provide tools for managing emotions and repairing relationships. Additionally, introspection, understanding, and learning from these experiences can contribute to personal growth and resilience. "Forgiveness is not always easy. At times, it feels more painful than the wound we suffered to forgive the one that inflicted it. And yet, there is no peace without forgiveness."— Marianne Williamson

While interpersonal offenses can substantially impact our well-being and relationships, our responses and ability to recover through forgiveness and reconciliation play a fundamental role in determining our overall happiness and the health of our connections with spouses. "When you forgive, you in no way change the past – but you sure do change the future." — Bernard Meltzer

Forgiveness looks different when we forgive a stranger versus a loved one. The cornerstone of a thriving marriage, forgiveness is pivotal for conflict resolution, relationship-enhancing attributions, and greater commitment. Forgiveness is a choice to pardon and love selflessly and is not dependent on justice or the offender admitting wrong.

Justice is not necessary for forgiveness. At the base of authentic forgiveness is unwavering love and patience. The Greek word for forgive is "Makrothumeo" and means to 'have patience with me; give me time'. Forgiveness is the positive response to a perception of injustice and often involves reconciliation. It can be both an internal and external process of resolving a conflict. In the context of marriage, forgiveness always accompanies reconciliation. There can be forgiveness without reconciliation, but there cannot be true reconciliation without forgiveness. Forgiveness must precede reconciliation for it to be effective.

Forgiveness is about the person doing the forgiving. Forgiveness within self allows for reconciliation within self, enabling forgiveness towards others and can lead to reconciliation. "To forgive is to set a prisoner free and discover that the prisoner was you."- Lewis B. Smedes

There are two primary ways to reconcile. These involves:

- implicit reconciliation.
- explicit reconciliation.

Implicit reconciliation occurs in relationships where forgiveness occurs almost automatically. In contrast, therapy generally aids explicit reconciliation and occurs when partners work together to reconcile by explicitly processing the issues. For explicit reconciliation to occur, hostilities must first be resolved. This is why nations in conflict declare a ceasefire as a prerequisite for discussions about future actions. Only if an agreement to put an end to hostilities is reached will progress be made toward reconciliation. Only then can the parties come together to work together.

Similarly, in marriages, couples sometimes must agree to a ceasefire with the help of a therapist or counsellor before pursuing peace. Feelings of anger, emotional pain, and the memory of the past often result in further hostility that will erode the foundation of the marriage. While managing your emotional outburst is paramount to accomplishing peace, merely ceasing hostile actions without interactions will not result in trust creation or relationship restoration. As soon as a truce violation occurs, the parties will immediately resume the conflict. Similarly, a reminder of past disappointment often leads to more fury and pain; therefore, a peaceful coming-together is essential. "Darkness cannot drive out darkness; only light can do that. Hate cannot drive out hate; only love can do that." — Martin Luther King, Jr.

Some years ago, a couple requested my help as they navigated the problematic tides in their marriage after I had just shared a comprehensive presentation about forgiveness and its importance through our weekly online devotion. I could hear the sobbing and feel the pain of a wife who was angry, disappointed, and harbouring thoughts of rejection. "I am mad, Rev. I love him, but truly he was dead. After all I have been through, how could he have treated me like this?" she reasoned. Jody has only been married for three years, and marriage has not been quite the exploits advertised by others. Her husband, Jack, has been abusive sexually, physically, and financially. He has been very insensitive to her emotional needs, but worst of all, he got involved with Jane, Jody's high school best friend. Jody was angry. She felt even more pain each time she thought about forgiving Jack. As I listened to her pour out her fury, I could not help but think: what would

Jesus do? Jody reminded me so much about Peter, one of Jesus' most outspoken disciples. How many times should one forgive? When is forgiveness too much? Jesus said we are to forgive others "seventy times seven" in response to Peter's question, "Lord, how many times shall I forgive my brother when he sins against me? Up to seven times?" —Matthew 18:21-22.

To gain a comprehensive analysis of what Jesus meant, we must explore the entire backstory. The Jewish rabbis at the time taught that forgiving someone more than three times was unnecessary, citing Amos 1:3-13 where God forgave Israel's enemies three times, then punished them. By offering forgiveness more than double that of the Old Testament example, Peter perhaps expected extra commendation from the Lord. When Jesus responded that forgiveness should be offered four hundred and ninety times, far beyond that which Peter was proposing, it must have stunned the disciples who were listening. Although they had been with Jesus for some time, they were still thinking in the limited terms of the law rather than in the unlimited terms of grace.

By saying we are to forgive those who sin against us seventy times seven, Jesus was not limiting forgiveness to 490 times, a number that is, for all practical purposes, beyond counting. Christians with forgiving hearts do not limit the number of times they forgive; they continue to forgive with as much grace the thousandth time as they do the first. Christians are only capable of this type of forgiving spirit because the Spirit of God lives within us, and it is He who provides the ability to offer forgiveness over and over, just as God forgives us.

Similarly, marriage, being the invention of God, can only be sustained by good forgivers. Forgiveness does not mean denial of the hurt felt or disappointment experienced, but instead, we make a conscious decision to pardon our spouse for the wrong done. It is not merit-based, neither must it be earned; it is the free gift we extend to our imperfect spouses while dismissing the charges for their imperfections. We do not receive it because we deserve it. It is that intentional decision we make to let go of the bonds of resentment and anger and the initial step we take to restore our relationship, renew trust, and heal broken wounds. Forgiveness does not mean denial of an act that caused hurt and disappointment; instead, quite the contrary. It lessens the grip it has on the offended and releases compassion for the offender. Forgiveness can be difficult, and some cases can be complicated, but forgiveness has a significant impact on the attitude and relationship of the forgiver. It can help release you from the control of the person who violated your expectations, allowing you to view each action or hurt as a mishandled input and a missed opportunity to treat you fairly. The hurt or pain caused was simply your spouse's choice and not a consequence of your action. You do not need to become an accomplice by levying like actions. Forgiveness is always the action of a responsible and optimistic individual. At times, forgiveness may lead to feelings of understanding, empathy, and compassion for the one who caused the hurt. This does not imply weakness; instead, it shows strength, setting aside your own hurt to consider your spouse's needs. Forgiveness requires us to consider our spouses' personal struggles and offer them grace.

As I spoke with Jody, I could visibly see that she was ready for a ceasefire. She was ready to consider Jack's errors while reflecting on her own imperfections. Becoming a good forgiver involves a conscious effort and a willingness to let go of negative feelings and resentment.

Here are some steps to help you become a better forgiver:

- **Understand the situation**

Take the time to understand what happened and how it made you feel. Acknowledge your emotions and the impact of the situation on you.

- **Empathise**

Try to understand the perspective of the person who wronged you. Empathy can help you see things from their point of view, which can make forgiveness easier.

- **Accept your feelings**

Accept that it's normal to feel hurt, angry, or upset. Don't suppress these emotions; work through them to achieve a sense of calm.

- **Let go of resentment**

Holding onto resentment only hurts you in the long run. Make a conscious decision to let go of the negative feelings associated with the situation.

- **Communicate (if appropriate)**

If the situation warrants it, communicate with the person who wronged you. Express your feelings constructively. Clear communication can aid in the process of forgiveness.

- **Practice self-compassion**

Be kind to yourself throughout this process. Forgiving doesn't mean forgetting, and it's okay to set boundaries or take time to heal.

- **Focus on the present**

Don't let the past control your present and future. Live in the present moment and work towards a future free from the weight of the past hurt.

- **Work on forgiveness daily**

Forgiveness is often a gradual process. To work on it daily, remind yourself of your commitment to forgive.

- **Seek support**

Sometimes, forgiveness is a challenging journey. If that's the case for you, consider seeking support from friends, family, a therapist, or a support group.

- **Reflect and learn**

Reflect on what you've learned from the situation. Forgiveness often brings valuable lessons and personal growth.

Dear couple,

Remember, forgiveness is a gift you give to yourself. It's a process that can lead to personal healing and peace of mind. Forgiveness doesn't necessarily mean reconciling with the person who hurt you, but it does mean releasing the situation's negative hold on your life.

While forgiveness does not always result in reconciliation, couples must strive to reconcile at all costs.

Reconciliation in marriage can be a complex and challenging process, but with commitment and effort from both partners, it's possible to rebuild and strengthen the relationship.

Here are some steps that may help in the process of reconciliation:

- **Communication**

Open, honest, and respectful communication is crucial. Listen to each other without interruption, and express your feelings, thoughts, and concerns openly. Try to understand each other's perspectives without judgment.

- **Identify issues**

Acknowledge the problems that led to the conflict. This might involve understanding the underlying reasons for the disagreement or hurt feelings. Addressing the root causes is important for genuine resolution.

- **Apologise and forgive**

It's important for both partners to take responsibility for their actions. Apologising sincerely for any mistakes or hurt caused and forgiving each other is essential for moving forward.

- **Seek counselling**

Consider couples therapy or marriage counselling. A professional therapist can provide guidance and support in resolving conflicts, improving communication, and understanding each other better.

- **Rebuild trust**

Trust might have been damaged, and it takes time to rebuild. To regain confidence, consistently demonstrate honesty, reliability, and commitment. Keep your promises and be transparent.

- **Work on common ground and solutions**

Find common ground and work together to find solutions that accommodate both partners' needs. Common ground is essential for resolving differences and reaching a middle ground.

- **Focus on the positive:**

Emphasize positive aspects of the relationship. Remind yourselves of the good times, shared values, and reasons you fell in love in the first place. This can help rekindle the emotional connection.

- **Give it time!**

Reconciliation is a process that takes time. Be patient and committed to the journey of healing and rebuilding your relationship. Rushing the process might lead to unresolved issues resurfacing later.

- **Self-reflection**

Reflect on your own behaviours and attitudes. Recognise where you might have contributed to the problems and work on self-improvement.

- **Set Boundaries and Expectations**

Establish clear boundaries and expectations for the relationship. Understanding and respecting each other's boundaries can help prevent future conflicts.

Dear couple,

Remember, reconciliation doesn't mean suppressing emotions or avoiding future disagreements. It's about dealing with issues in a constructive and healthy way, learning from past mistakes, and moving forward together as a stronger, more resilient couple. If the issues seem too complex to handle on your own, seeking professional help is always a good option.

Reflect Now That You Have Proceeded...

Circle the flag light that best describes your assessment of yourself/ partner based on the topic: **Marriage, Forgiveness and Reconciliation.**

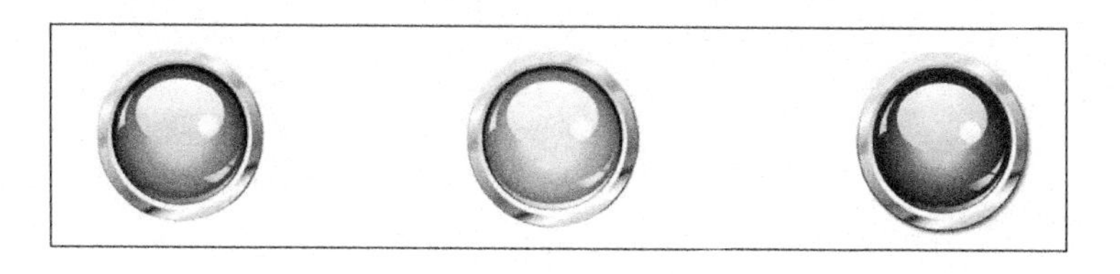

Explain your answer based your previous selection:

Know-Metre: Now appraise your knowledge of this topic after reading by circling the gauge.

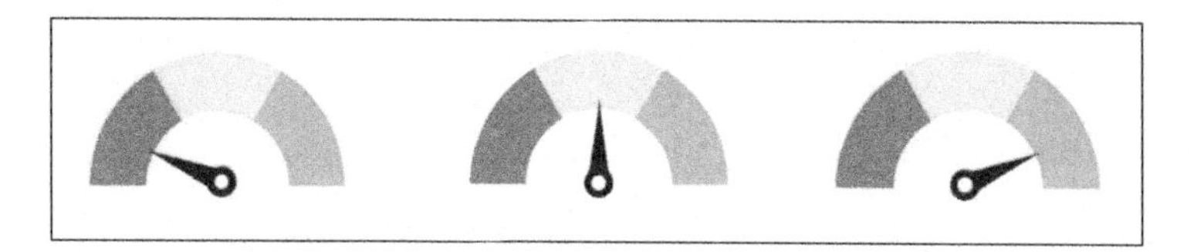

MARRIAGE, SUPPORT AND PARTNERSHIP

The Power of Partnership: Cultivating a Strong Partnership Within Marriage

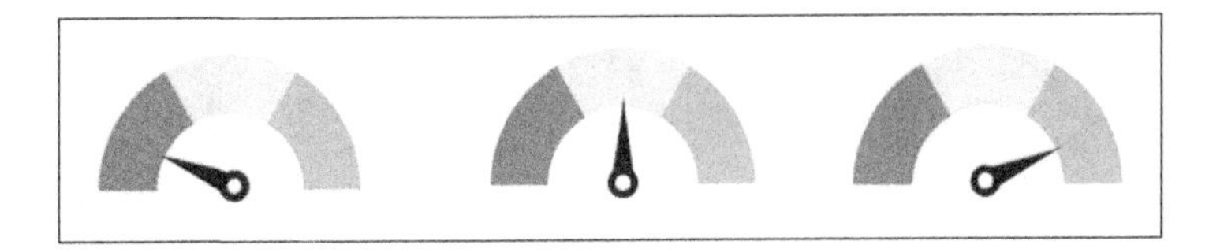

"The goal in marriage is not to think alike, but to think together." — Robert C. Dodds

A partnership within marriage signifies a dynamic, collaborative relationship between spouses. Partnership in marriage encapsulates the essence of collaboration, unity, and mutual support between spouses. It's the cornerstone upon which a strong and enduring relationship is built—a dynamic interplay of shared responsibilities, aspirations, and decisions. In this partnership, each individual brings their unique strengths, perspectives, and contributions, creating a synergy that fosters growth and resilience. It involves a commitment to walk side by side, facing life's challenges as a team, and cherishing moments of triumph together. This collaborative bond thrives on open communication, compromise, and a deep-seated respect for each other's autonomy, cultivating an environment where both partners feel valued, understood, and empowered to navigate the complexities of life as a unified force. Partnership within marriage involves mutual support, collaboration, and shared decision-making. It's a commitment to working together as a team. The partners share responsibilities, both in day-to-day tasks and in major life decisions. It's about working together to achieve common goals. A strong partnership in marriage builds strength and resilience within the relationship. Partners face challenges together and support each other through thick and thin. Partnership promotes open and effective communication. Discussing goals, concerns, and decisions together fosters a sense of unity.

Respecting each other's opinions, feelings, and contributions is essential in nurturing a partnership. Acknowledging and appreciating each other's efforts strengthens the bond.

Partners should align their goals and aspirations. Discussing shared visions helps to work towards common objectives and maintain a sense of direction. They should share the responsibilities, adjusting to each other's strengths and limitations. Dividing tasks based on each other's abilities fosters a balanced partnership. Being a supportive partner involves offering encouragement, assistance, and understanding in each other's endeavours, further strengthening the partnership. Partnerships thrive on problem-solving together. Facing challenges as a team, finding solutions, and supporting each other builds a resilient partnership. Recognising and respecting each other's individuality and differences fosters a sense of partnership. Partners appreciate their differences and work together despite them.

Dear couple,

A strong partnership within marriage involves teamwork, support, shared goals, and effective communication. Couples can build a robust and enduring partnership by fostering collaboration, mutual respect, and a shared vision.

Remember, the commitment to working together, supporting each other, and facing challenges as a team fortifies the marital relationship, creating a strong and lasting union built on trust, cooperation, and mutual respect. Support in marriage is the sturdy pillar that sustains and uplifts the relationship, nurturing an environment of understanding, empathy, and unwavering encouragement. It's a profound commitment to stand by each other through the highs and lows, offering a comforting embrace in times of distress and celebrating victories with boundless enthusiasm. This support manifests in myriad forms—be it emotional, physical, or psychological—where spouses become each other's rock, providing solace, guidance, and a safe haven in the storms of life. It involves actively listening, validating feelings, and offering a helping hand without judgment or reservation. Ultimately, the essence of support in marriage lies in fostering an atmosphere where both partners feel unconditionally accepted, respected, and empowered to flourish as individuals within the sanctity of their shared union.

Reflect Now That You Have Proceeded...

Circle the flag light that best describes your assessment of yourself/ partner based on the topic: **Marriage and Partnership.**

Explain your answer based your previous selection:

Know-Metre: Now appraise your knowledge of this topic after reading by circling the gauge.

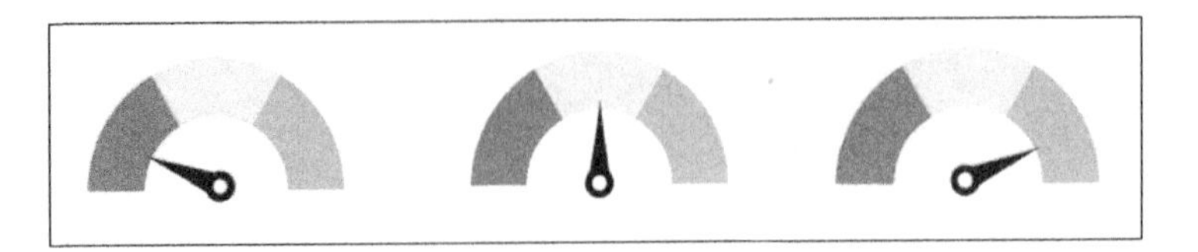

MARRIAGE AND MONEY

The Divine Partnership of Marriage and Financial Responsibility

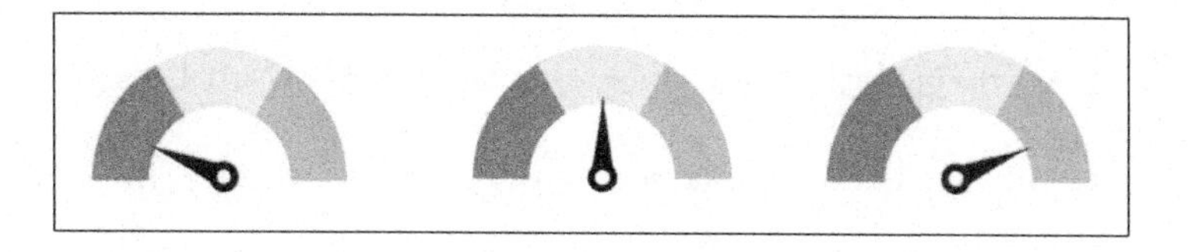

"Money is only a tool. It will take you wherever you wish, but it will not replace you as the driver." – Ayn Rand

In the sanctity of marriage, the union of two individuals is not only a spiritual and emotional bond but also an intertwining of lives, including the management of finances. Money, often a sensitive topic, plays a significant role in the health and stability of a marital relationship. It's within the framework of faith, love, and shared principles that couples can navigate financial matters, aligning their beliefs with practical stewardship.

Money as a tool, not a master

Understanding the biblical perspective on money is foundational. The Scriptures teach that wealth and possessions, while necessary for sustenance, should not govern or control our lives. Instead, they are to be seen as resources to be managed wisely. In marriage, financial resources are considered a gift from God to be used responsibly and for the betterment of the family, the community, and God's Kingdom.

Couples should diligently work, save conscientiously, and secure health and life insurance to shield their family from overwhelming debts. In addition to these measures, cultivating and practicing sound spending habits is crucial.

Here are some critical practices:

- **Mutual accountability and transparency**

Open communication regarding financial matters is vital. Both partners should actively participate in financial decisions, aligning their priorities and goals. Honesty, transparency, and mutual accountability form the bedrock of a healthy financial relationship within marriage. This includes discussing income, expenses, savings, debts, and long-term aspirations. Such openness fosters trust and unity in managing the family's finances.

- **Stewardship and generosity**

A central tenet in Christian teachings is the concept of stewardship. This principle emphasizes that individuals are stewards or caretakers of God's resources. In a marital context, this means responsible management of finances, using them wisely to serve God's purposes and the needs of others. Giving generously and supporting charitable causes not only reflects Christian values but also strengthens the marital bond by fostering a shared sense of purpose and contribution to the greater good.

- **Budgeting and financial planning**

Developing a budget and financial plan is a practical step in managing money in a marriage. A budget guides spending, savings, and investments, ensuring financial stability and preventing conflicts. Setting mutual financial goals and regularly reviewing and adjusting the budget together can reinforce the partnership and mutual commitment to a shared financial future. It is developing and adhering to a budget that serves as a forward-looking plan for spending money. This is a valuable tool in managing finances, offering a comprehensive overview of financial obligations, and serving as a guide for fulfilment.

- **Overcoming challenges and conflicts**

Financial disagreements are common in marriages. They can stem from differing money mindsets, spending habits, or unexpected circumstances. Addressing these conflicts with patience, empathy, and respect for each other's perspectives is crucial. Seeking counsel from a trusted spiritual advisor or financial planner can offer guidance in resolving differences and strengthening the financial aspect of the marital relationship.

In a Christian marriage, money is not merely a matter of practicality, but an aspect deeply intertwined with spiritual beliefs and values. When approached with mutual respect, transparency, and a shared commitment to biblical principles of stewardship, finances can be a unifying force, enhancing the strength and longevity of the marital bond.

- **Manage cash flow**

Cash flow, the net amount of cash and equivalents entering and leaving an account, requires prudent control of income and expenditures. Regular assessment of financial standing and the application of disciplined measures are essential. Recognizing that cash devalues over time due to inflation while assets appreciate prompts the need to seek opportunities to increase income actively. This may involve investments in REITs, stocks, and bonds, aiming to earn more while spending less. As assets grow, the acquired profit can be utilised to meet essential family needs such as housing, transportation, food, education, healthcare, utilities, and clothing.

Dear couple,

Remember, the journey of financial stewardship in a Christian marriage is a process that requires dedication, understanding, and prayer. By aligning financial decisions with faith, couples can navigate the complexities of money management, strengthening their relationship and honouring their commitment to God and each other.

Register for the IOBI transformative course, "Critical Keys for Financial Freedom," for a more in-depth understanding of achieving financial success." Tailored to man's financial needs, this course provides:

- Essential, step-by-step, practical, workable, and Biblical keys for increasing income.
- Enhancing value.
- Wealth creation.
- Managing debt and cash flow.

Details for purchase are available at the end of this book.

Reflect Now That You Have Proceeded...

Circle the flag light that best describes your assessment of yourself/ partner based on the topic: **Marriage and Conflict management.**

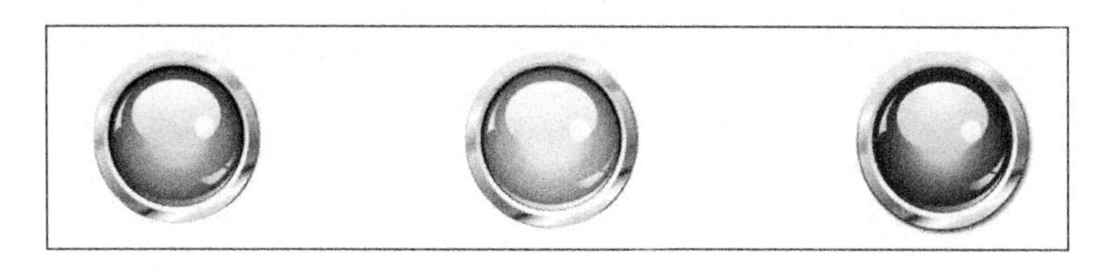

Explain your answer based your previous selection:

Know-Metre: Now appraise your knowledge of this topic after reading by circling the gauge.

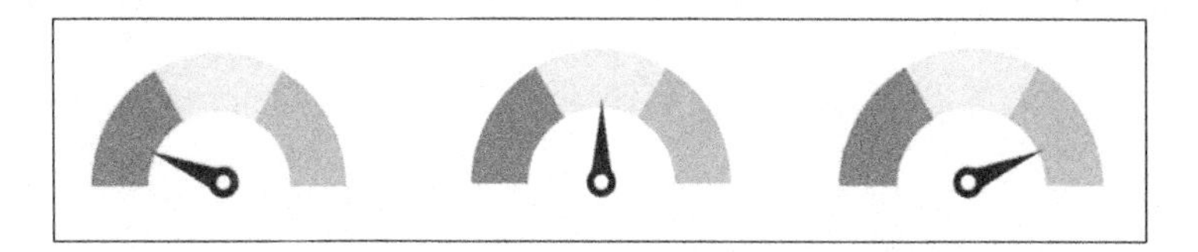

MARRIAGE AND CONFLICT MANAGEMENT

Understanding and Managing Conflict in Marital Relationships

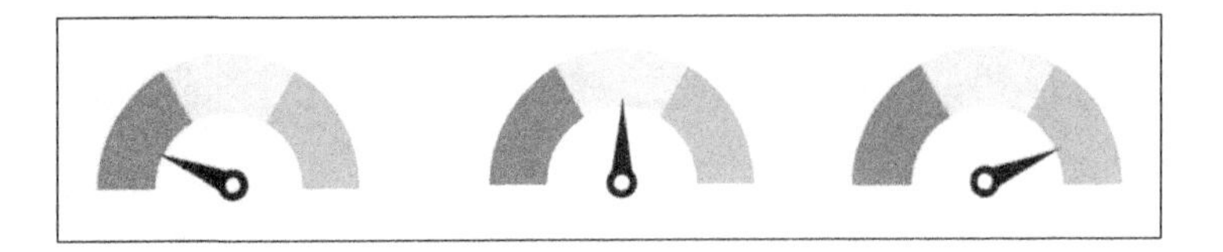

"What counts in making a happy marriage is not so much how compatible you are, but how you deal with incompatibility." — Leo Tolstoy

Conflict is an inevitable part of any relationship, including marriage. How couples navigate and resolve conflict significantly impacts the health and longevity of a union. Conflict management is crucial to interpersonal dynamics, marital success, and harmony. Effectively handling conflicts involves understanding diverse perspectives, promoting open communication, and seeking mutually beneficial resolutions. Employing active listening and empathy fosters a conducive environment for addressing underlying issues.

Additionally, embracing collaborative problem-solving approaches encourages cooperation rather than confrontation. Successful conflict management not only resolves immediate disputes, it also contributes to a positive and resilient social fabric, promoting growth and understanding among couples.

Acknowledging the nature of conflict

Conflicts arise due to partners' differing perspectives, values, needs, and expectations. It's crucial to understand that conflict itself isn't negative; rather, how couples address and resolve it determines its impact on the relationship. Instead of avoiding conflict, embracing it as an opportunity for growth can lead to deeper understanding and stronger bonds.

Effective communication as the foundation

Open, honest, and respectful communication is the cornerstone of conflict management. Active listening, allowing each partner to express their thoughts and emotions without interruption, and seeking to understand before being understood are key components. It's vital to communicate with empathy. We must avoid attacking or blaming language to foster a safe environment for discussion.

Identifying and addressing root causes

During conflicts, it's often easy to focus on the surface issue rather than the underlying cause. Understanding the root of the problem—unmet needs, past experiences, or miscommunication—is essential for resolving conflicts effectively. Taking time to identify these root causes can lead to more meaningful and lasting resolutions.

Constructive conflict resolution techniques

Several techniques can be employed to manage conflicts constructively:

- ***Compromise and collaboration:*** Finding a middle ground where both partners' needs are met is crucial. This requires a willingness to give and take, emphasizing the "we" rather than "me" mentality.

- ***Time-outs and reflection:*** Sometimes, taking a break from a heated discussion can provide space for reflection, preventing further escalation. Agreeing to pause and resume the conversation when emotions have cooled can be immensely beneficial.

- ***Seeking mediation or counselling:*** In cases where conflicts persist or seem insurmountable, seeking the help of a neutral third party, such as a counsellor or mediator, can offer a fresh perspective and guidance.

Forgiveness and moving forward

Forgiveness is a pivotal aspect of conflict resolution in marriage. Acknowledging mistakes, seeking, and granting forgiveness, and letting go of resentment are crucial for moving forward. It's not about forgetting the issue, but instead releasing the negative emotions associated with it and committing to rebuilding trust.

Cultivating a culture of respect and grace

Respecting each other's differences, recognising that conflict is a natural part of growth, and extending grace toward one another during challenging times are key components of a healthy conflict management strategy. Learning to disagree without disrespect is a foundational principle in resolving conflicts.

Dear couple,

Conflict is an inevitable part of any marriage. However, it can be a catalyst for growth, understanding, and strengthening the bond between partners when approached constructively. By implementing effective communication, understanding the root causes, and embracing forgiveness, couples can navigate conflicts gracefully, leading to a stronger, more resilient marital relationship. Remember, it's not the absence of conflict but how it is managed that determines the strength of a marriage.

Reflect Now That You Have Proceeded...

Circle the flag light that best describes your assessment of yourself/ partner based on the topic: **Marriage and Conflict Management.**

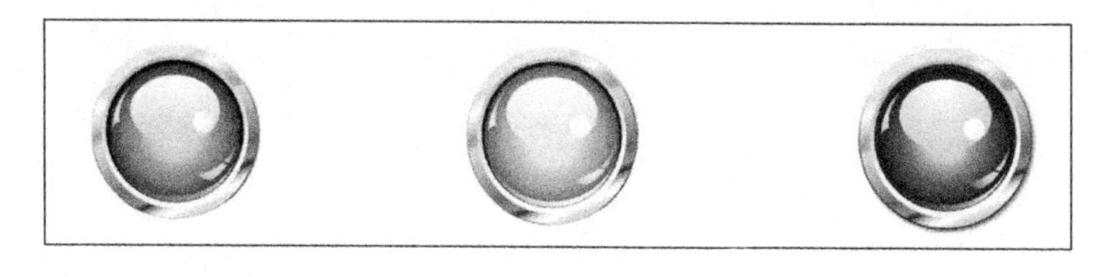

Explain your answer based your previous selection:

Know-Metre: Now appraise your knowledge of this topic after reading by circling the gauge.

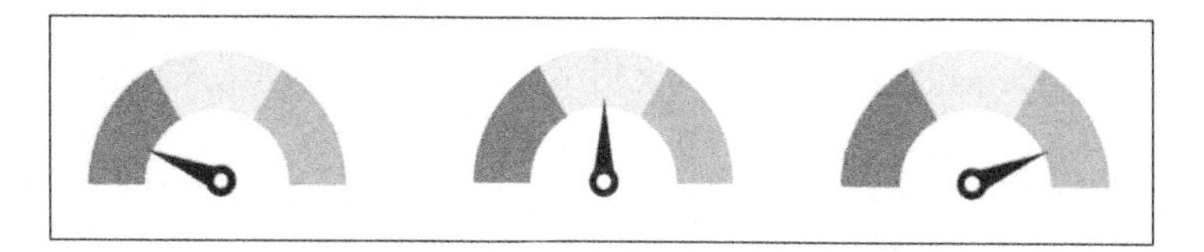

MARRIAGE AND FIDELITY

Upholding Trust and Fidelity in Marital Relationships

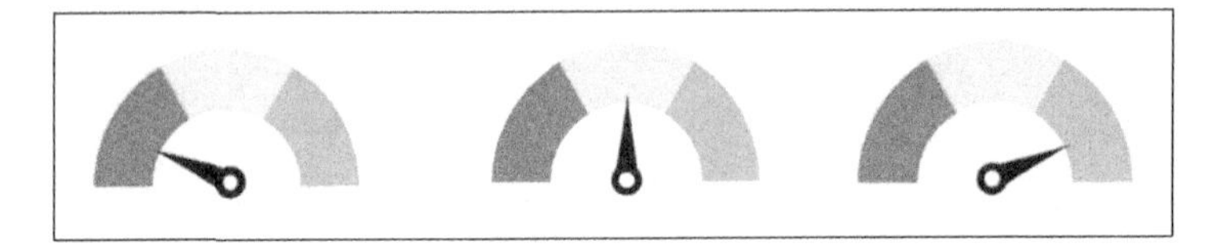

"Success in marriage does not come merely through finding the right mate, but through being the right mate."

— Barnett R. Bricker

Marriage is a sacred union, a commitment that extends beyond the bounds of romantic connection. Fidelity, a cornerstone of a thriving marriage, embodies the loyalty and trust between partners. It goes beyond mere physical exclusivity, delving into emotional and mental faithfulness. Maintaining fidelity in marriage requires open communication, understanding, and a shared dedication to weathering the storms together in a world marked by constant change. It is the conscious choice to prioritise the relationship, nurturing a bond that withstands the trials of time. Fidelity is not just a promise; it's a continuous, intentional act that solidifies the foundation of a lasting and meaningful marital connection.

Fidelity in marriage goes beyond the physical act of remaining faithful. It includes emotional faithfulness, trustworthiness, and a steadfast commitment to the well-being and exclusivity of the relationship. It is an oath of loyalty, honesty, and the choice to prioritise and honour the marriage above all else.

A marriage founded on fidelity cultivates a deep sense of security, trust, and emotional intimacy between partners. When both individuals commit to exclusivity, it fosters an environment where each person feels safe, valued, and respected. The bond strengthens as couples share their lives, dreams, and vulnerabilities in a space of unwavering trust.

Open, transparent communication is a crucial element in upholding fidelity. Couples should feel comfortable discussing their feelings, needs, and concerns openly.

Creating an environment where both partners feel heard and understood helps strengthen the emotional connection, reducing the likelihood of seeking emotional intimacy outside the marriage.

Transparency in actions and interactions will reinforce trust in a marriage. This involves being open about friendships, daily activities, and interactions without the need for secrecy. Both partners should feel secure knowing they can trust each other completely. Undoubtedly, fidelity might face challenges, particularly when faced with temptations or external stressors. Being aware of potential risks and actively setting boundaries can help navigate these challenges. Therefore, we must understand our vulnerabilities, discuss concerns openly, and work together to maintain a robust and resilient bond.

Regularly reaffirming commitment and nurturing the relationship helps to uphold fidelity. Date nights, shared activities, reaffirming vows, and prioritising the relationship amid life's demands are prime examples. When both partners invest time and effort into the marriage, it strengthens the foundation of fidelity.

Dear couple,

Fidelity is a sacred commitment in marriage, central to the relationship's trust, intimacy, and longevity. Upholding fidelity requires continuous effort, communication, and mutual respect. By prioritising the bond between partners and actively fostering an environment of trust and transparency, couples can nurture a relationship built on the solid foundation of unwavering fidelity. Remember, fidelity is not merely a promise but a continual choice to honour and cherish the commitment made to each other.

Reflect Now That You Have Proceeded...

Circle the flag light that best describes your assessment of yourself/ partner based on the topic: **Marriage and Fidelity**

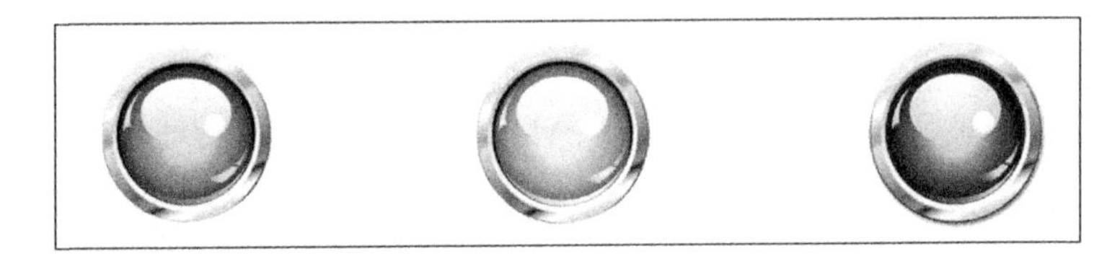

Explain your answer based your previous selection:

Know-Metre: Now appraise your knowledge of this topic after reading by circling the gauge.

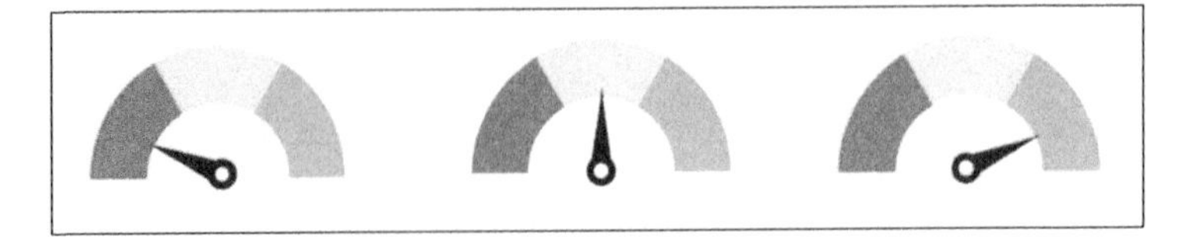

MARRIAGE AND GOAL ATTAINMENT

Aligning Aspirations and Cultivating Growth in Marital Relationships

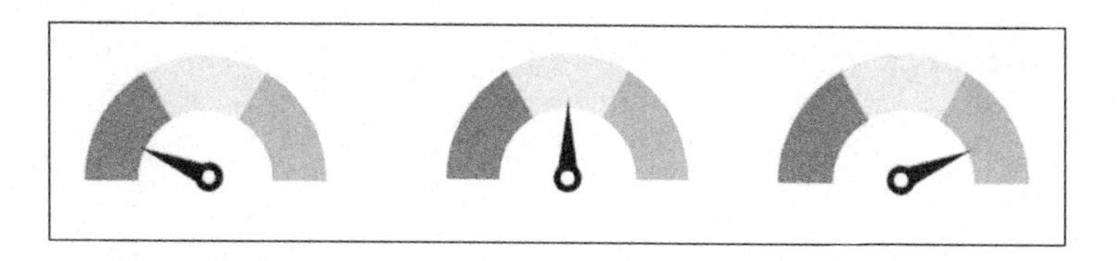

"A great marriage is something that just happens; it's something that must be created." — Unknown

Goal attainment in marriage is akin to navigating a shared journey toward mutual aspirations. It involves aligning individual ambitions and collective dreams, fostering a harmonious balance between personal growth and the unity of partnership. Achieving goals in marriage encompasses diverse facets—be it career milestones, family aspirations, or personal development. It thrives on communication, collaboration, and unwavering support, where partners become each other's champions, providing encouragement and solidarity along the way. It's about celebrating shared successes, navigating challenges together, and constantly evolving as a team while honouring each other's unique aspirations. In essence, goal attainment in marriage signifies the fusion of individual aspirations into a collective vision, forging a path filled with understanding, support, and shared triumphs.

Setting and working toward shared goals in a marriage helps to create a sense of purpose and direction. Having common objectives cultivates unity and strengthens marital bonds, whether financial, career, family, personal, or spiritual. Couples find joy and motivation in celebrating joint accomplishments.

To set and pursue goals effectively, facilitating open and transparent communication is essential. Couples ought to discuss each other's dreams, aspirations, and priorities; establishing clear, attainable, and measurable goals allows for mutual understanding and shared commitment to the journey. In addition to shared goals, supporting each other's individual growth is equally important. Encouraging personal aspirations and providing support in individual pursuits fosters an environment of respect and understanding. It allows both partners to grow as individuals while enhancing the relationship.

As established earlier in this manual, conflicts in marriage are inevitable and can sometimes arise from our goals or aspirations due to differing perspectives or priorities. Finding a balance between individual and shared goals is therefore critical. Through respectful communication, commonplace, and understanding, couples can find ways to support each other's aspirations without compromising the unity of the relationship.

Accountability plays a vital role in achieving goals. Partners must hold each other accountable, provide support, and collaborate to pursue shared objectives. Regular check-ins, discussions, and adjustments to the established plan will foster staying on track and adapting to life's changes. The path to goal attainment in marriage may not always be smooth. Challenges, setbacks, and unexpected turns are natural. Facing these obstacles as a team, learning from failures, and celebrating small victories along the way are crucial for staying motivated and resilient.

Dear couple,

Setting and achieving goals in marriage strengthens the relationship and the individuals within it. Through clear communication, support for individual growth, and a commitment to shared aspirations, couples can grow closer while pursuing their dreams. Remember, working together toward shared goals fortifies the marital bond and creates a fulfilling, purpose-driven journey.

For a more detailed analysis of this topic, consider getting the book "Before You Say I Do: 21 Considerations to Ponder Before Constructing a Marriage.

Reflect Now That You Have Proceeded...

Circle the flag light that best describes your assessment of yourself/ partner based on the topic: **Marriage and Goal Attainment.**

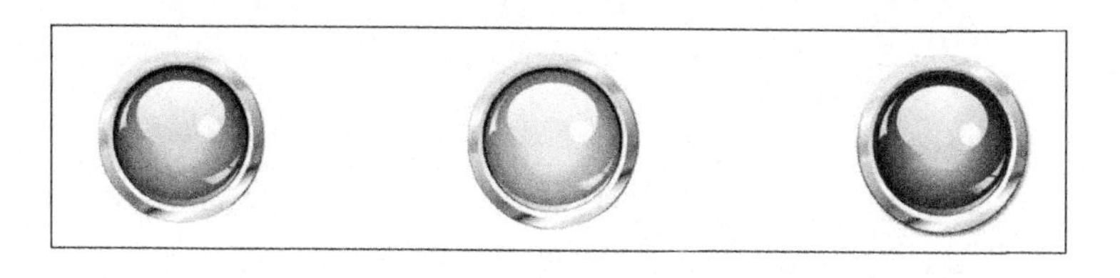

Explain your answer based your previous selection:

Know-Metre: Now appraise your knowledge of this topic after reading by circling the gauge.

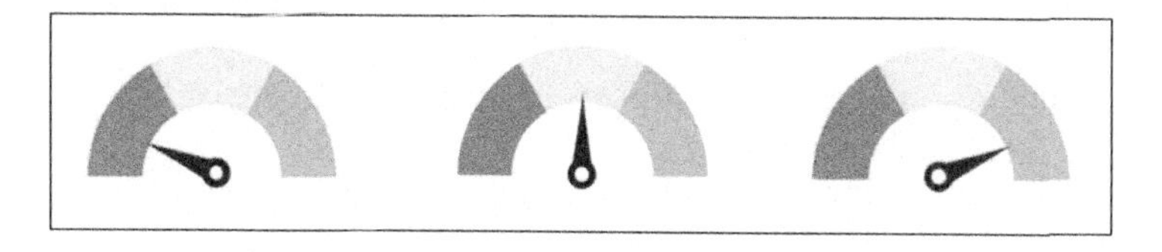

MARRIAGE AND FAITH

Nurturing the Sacred Connection in Marital Relationships

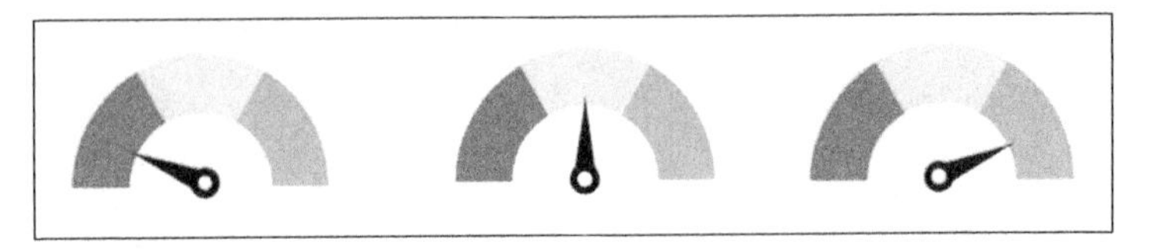

"There is no more lovely, friendly and charming relationship, communion or company than a good marriage."

— Martin Luther

Marriage and faith often intertwine, fostering a profound bond anchored in shared beliefs and values. For many, faith is vital in their marital journey, providing a moral compass and guiding principles that shape their relationship. It can offer a framework for navigating challenges, fostering forgiveness, and nurturing a sense of commitment and loyalty. Couples often draw strength from their shared faith, finding solace and support in times of adversity and joy. Moreover, faith can infuse rituals, traditions, and spiritual practices into the fabric of the relationship, deepening emotional intimacy and providing a sense of purpose and meaning beyond the individual selves.

Shared faith and spiritual beliefs create a strong foundation in a marriage. When partners share a common belief system, it fosters unity, understanding, and a sense of purpose. Having a shared faith provides a guiding principle to help navigate challenges, provide strength, and build resilience within the relationship. Beyond the emotional and physical aspects, the spiritual connection between partners can deepen intimacy. Sharing spiritual practices, beliefs, and prayers can strengthen the bond and provide a unique form of closeness, enabling both partners to connect on a profound, soulful level.

In a marriage where faith is central, the shared values and beliefs serve as a pilot in decision-making. Aligning choices with these values will aid the resolution of conflicts and the making of important life decisions together.

Faith often serves as a source of strength during challenging times. It provides hope, comfort, and a sense of resilience when navigating hardships. Believing in something greater than oneself can offer solace and a broader perspective, helping couples weather life's storms together.

Incorporating spiritual practices together, such as prayer, meditation, attending religious services, or engaging in acts of service, can deepen the spiritual connection between partners. These practices foster personal growth and will enhance the connection shared between partners within the marriage.

Undeniably, in some marriages, partners might have differing faith backgrounds or beliefs. Respect and understanding of each other's beliefs are essential in such situations. Open communication, empathy, and a willingness to learn from each other's faith traditions can enrich the relationship.

Dear couple,

Faith in marriage provides a solid framework for a deeper, more profound connection between partners. It fosters unity, provides strength during challenges, and offers a guiding light for shared values and decision-making. Embracing and nurturing this spiritual aspect in marriage can significantly enhance our bond and create a relationship deeply rooted in shared beliefs and values. Remember, it's the mutual respect, shared practices, and continual cultivation of the spiritual connection that enriches the journey of marriage.

Reflect Now That You Have Proceeded...

Circle the flag light that best describes your assessment of yourself/ partner based on the topic: **Marriage and Faith.**

Explain your answer based your previous selection:

Know-Metre: Now appraise your knowledge of this topic after reading by circling the gauge.

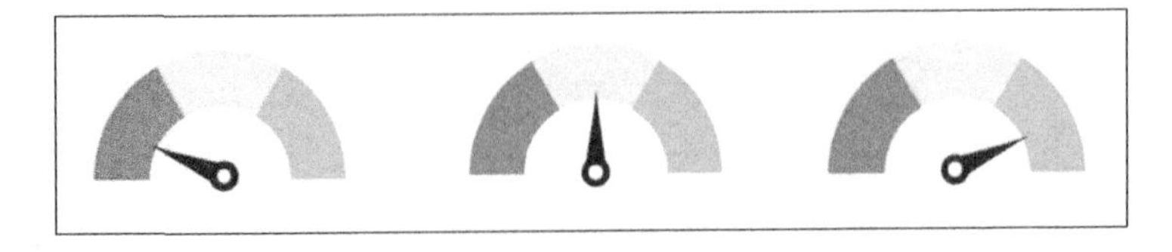

MARRIAGE AND GENDER ROLES

Redefining Gender Roles: Evolving Dynamics in Marital Relationships

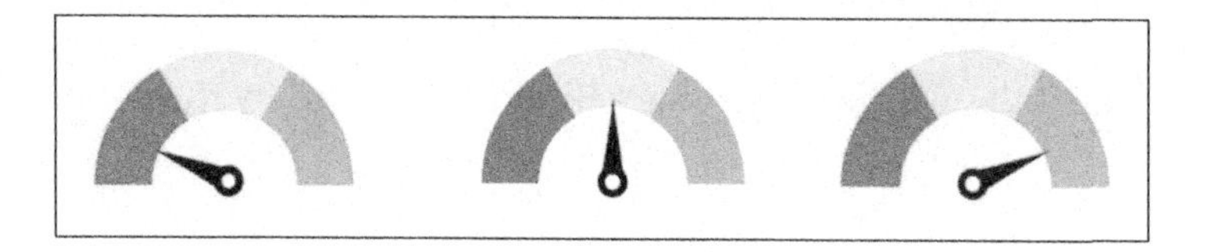

"The great marriages are partnerships. It can't be a great marriage without being a partnership." — Helen Mirren

Contemporary marriages often embrace flexibility in gender roles, allowing couples to define responsibilities based on individual strengths, preferences, and circumstances rather than predetermined societal expectations. Many couples opt for a more equal distribution of tasks, from financial contributions to household chores and childcare, seeking balance and shared responsibilities.

Yet, some couples find fulfilment in more traditional roles, choosing to divide responsibilities according to conventional gender norms. The essence of modern marriage lies in the freedom to negotiate and redefine these roles based on mutual understanding and respect rather than adhering strictly to predefined societal standards. The key is open communication, mutual consent, and the recognition that the roles within a marriage should be defined by the couple's needs and aspirations rather than external pressures or expectations.

Indeed, modern marriages often challenge traditional gender roles. The notion of predefined roles for men and women within a relationship is giving way to a more fluid, flexible approach. Couples are redefining these roles based on mutual agreement, individual strengths, and personal preferences.

In contemporary marriages, the concept of equality is prominent. Partners often share financial contributions, household chores, childcare, and decision-making responsibilities. There's a growing emphasis on equal partnership, where both individuals have an active role in all aspects of the relationship. The changing dynamics in gender roles have brought about a more flexible and adaptable approach. Couples adjust their roles based on strengths, interests, and the demands of the situation. This adaptability allows for a more harmonious and cooperative partnership.

Communication is critical in redefining gender roles within marriage. Open discussions about each partner's preferences, strengths, and aspirations help define comfortable and satisfying roles for both individuals. Mutual agreement and support are crucial in this process; however, there must be respect for individuality and choice. Both partners must be free to pursue their interests and goals outside of traditional gender roles. Mutual support for individual aspirations fosters a stronger, more satisfying relationship.

Transitioning from traditional gender roles to more fluid ones can pose challenges. Conflicts might arise due to societal expectations or personal beliefs. Addressing these conflicts through open dialogue and mutual understanding is crucial for navigating the evolving dynamics.

Dear spouse,

The evolution of gender roles in marriages reflects a broader societal shift towards equality and partnership. Embracing flexibility, open communication, and mutual respect for individual choices allows couples to create a more harmonious, fulfilling relationship. Remember, mutual agreement, adaptability, and support for each other's preferences will foster a more balanced and satisfying marital relationship in today's changing landscape.

Christian marriages often look to biblical teachings for guidance on various aspects, including the roles of husbands and wives within the union. The scriptural perspectives on gender roles in Christian marriages entail understanding the principles of mutual respect, love, and partnership as depicted in the Bible. The ensuing are the biblical guides.

Foundational biblical principles

The Bible offers guidance on the roles of husbands and wives within Christian marriage. Ephesians 5:22-33 emphasises mutual submission, love, and respect. The passage advocates for husbands to love their wives sacrificially, as Christ loved the church, and for wives to submit to their husbands in a loving, respectful manner.

Mutual submission and respect

The biblical view of marriage emphasises mutual submission and respect between spouses. It's important to note that the call for wives to submit is not about inferiority but rather an order that reflects Christ's sacrificial love and the Church's response. Both partners are called to honour and support one another.

Leadership and servant-hood

The Bible emphasises the husband's role as the head of the household. However, this concept is often misinterpreted. The biblical leadership model for husbands is not one of dominance but of sacrificial love and servant leadership. Husbands are encouraged to love their wives unconditionally and sacrificially, mirroring Christ's love for the Church.

Partnership in decision making

While the Bible outlines the husband's role as the head of the household, it's important to recognise that decision-making is not unilateral. Biblical principles encourage husbands and wives to work together in making decisions, respecting each other's opinions, and seeking solutions that honour God and benefit the family.

Unique gifts and responsibilities

The Bible acknowledges that both spouses have unique gifts and strengths. Christian marriages encourage each partner to use their gifts to benefit the family and the glory of God. Honouring and supporting each other in their unique roles and responsibilities within the marriage is essential.

Respecting individual dignity

Christian teachings emphasise the inherent dignity and worth of each individual. In a Christian marriage, respect, honour, and love for each other should be paramount, recognising the value each partner brings to the relationship.

Dear couple,

Marriage, guided by biblical principles, emphasises mutual respect, sacrificial love, and partnership. Understanding and embodying these principles is essential, recognizing the value of mutual submission, respect, and love in building a strong, God-honouring marital relationship. Remember, mutual love, respect, and commitment to biblical principles form the foundation of a fulfilling Christian marriage.

For a more detailed analysis, consider getting the book Before You Say I Do 21 Considerations to Ponder Before Constructing a Marriage.

Reflect Now That You Have Proceeded...

Circle the flag light that best describes your assessment of yourself/ partner based on the topic: **Marriage and Gender Roles.**

Explain your answer based your previous selection:

Know-Metre: Now appraise your knowledge of this topic after reading by circling the gauge.

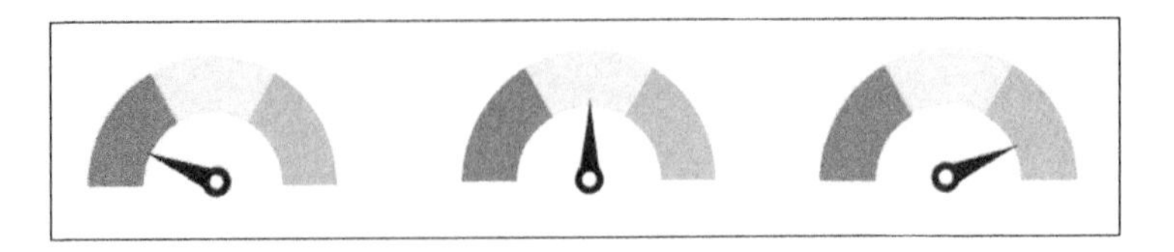

MARRIAGE AND HEADSHIP

Navigating Headship in Marriage: Exploring Roles, Communication and Leadership for Lasting Connection.

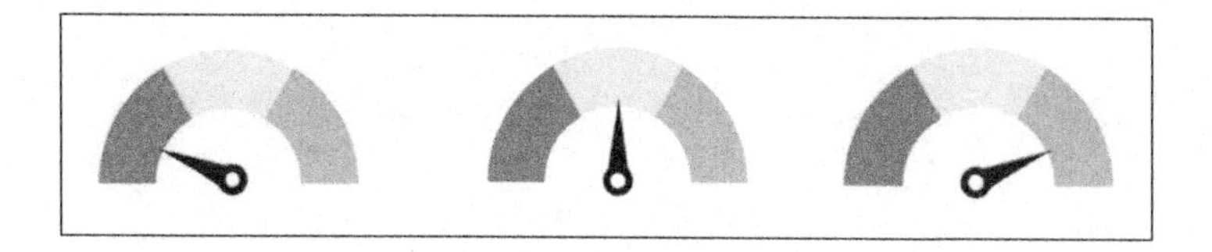

"True headship is not about dominance, but a humble and loving commitment to guide, protect, and uplift your partner on the shared journey of life." —Unknown

The concept of a "head" embodies the origin from which proper organisation and arrangement stem. It inherently represents a source of guidance and structure. It is employed metaphorically to illustrate a man's role in relation to his wife. The principle of male leadership is evident in the detailed account of the creation of man and woman in Genesis 1 and 2. Genesis 1 illustrates that both man and woman were created in the image of God. God's intention was for them to govern the earth for His purposes, following His example. It's crucial to recognise that the image of God and His plan for humanity's dominion encompassed both males and females.

Male leadership within the household is seen as something intrinsic. Through God's sovereign act of creation, husbands play a crucial role in shaping the dynamics of their homes. Essentially, their inherent nature spills over, significantly influencing the atmosphere within the household. Consequently, men are called by God to provide what their homes need to align with God's intentions. However, whether done cruelly or kindly, passively, or aggressively, this shaping occurs and reflects the essence of the husband. This inherent aspect of masculinity holds profound implications, a weighty reality to acknowledge.

We must admit that the presence of evil complicates the concept of headship for humanity. While headship exists within the Godhead and among the angels without abuse, evil inclines humans to exploit it for personal advantage, particularly within marriage.

The responsibility of being a head entails husbands turning away from self-determination and toward submission to Jesus Christ, who becomes the ultimate leader and exemplar for all actions. This shift involves moving away from self-centeredness and embracing sacrificial love, transitioning from an authoritarian style to a more relational form of leadership. It's a call to establish an environment characterised by truth and honesty. The headship of husbands can only occur where there is submission of wives; it cannot occur without submission.

Biblical teachings, particularly Ephesians 5:22-33 and other verses mention the concept of the husband as the head of the household. This concept, often associated with headship, concerns a husband's role in loving his wife sacrificially and leading the family in a manner that mirrors Christ's love for the Church.

The concept of headship emphasises a model of leadership rooted in servanthood. Rather than dominance or control, the biblical model calls for husbands to lead by loving and serving their wives, just as Christ loved and served the Church. Biblical teachings on headship also emphasise mutual submission and respect between spouses. While the husband leads the family, the wife submits respectfully and lovingly, mirroring the Church's response to Christ's sacrificial love.

Headship in marriage, as outlined biblically, doesn't imply unilateral decision-making. Instead, it promotes the idea of making decisions together, with the husband taking the lead while considering and respecting his wife's input. This encourages unity and mutual respect in the processes. While the husband may have a leadership role in the family, both spouses have complementary but equally valuable roles. Each partner brings unique strengths, gifts, and perspectives to the marriage, contributing to its well-being. Headship is with equality, shared decision-making, and mutual respect. Many contemporary Christian couples understand headship as a call to lovingly lead and serve, with both partners equally contributing to the marriage's success.

Dear couple,

The concept of headship in marriage, rooted in biblical teachings, promotes unity, sacrificial love, and mutual respect. It's about recognising and embodying the responsibility of leadership with humility, servanthood, and love, while fostering a sense of unity and partnership within the marriage. Embracing this principle in a modern context allows couples to navigate their marital journey with mutual respect, understanding, and a shared commitment to the family's well-being.

In marriage, a man's authority isn't self-assumed but rooted in Biblical guidance. It's not about his strength or wisdom but a divine appointment. This authority must align with Scripture. It's stated that the 'husband is the head of the wife, as Christ is the head of the church', emphasising a love akin to Christ's for the church, sacrificing for it (Eph. 5:23-25). This sacrificial love should be central for husbands, making it easier for wives to embrace submission to a loving partner. It's not about dominance but gentle leadership, seeking the wife's benefit.

Leadership isn't about commanding from a throne or treating a wife as inferior. The husband should expect responsibilities from his wife but participate eagerly in shared tasks. Leading means being selfless, mirroring Christ's self-denial and sacrificial love.

The husband's love should reflect Christ's sacrifice for the church. Family standards should align with Scripture, and it's the husband's role to maintain them. Studying and applying the Bible diligently is vital. As the head, he's responsible for the family's education, ensuring alignment with biblical principles and encouraging his wife's pursuit of wisdom. In raising children, the father should leverage the mother's talents, especially with younger children. His duties include enforcing rules, correcting wrongs, discouraging worldly behaviour, gossip, and slander. Discipline should come from love, patience, and the Word of God. Fathers should discipline, often with the mother's involvement.

Remember that demonstrating meekness, humility, holiness, and piety earns respect and authority. Consistency between words and actions is crucial, avoiding hypocrisy that weakens leadership. Providing for the family is primarily the husband's responsibility, but the wife may contribute financially without compromising family care. Protecting the family—spiritually, mentally, and physically—is the husband's duty.

The husband's role is to lead the family in prayer for their well-being and salvation. As head of the household, he is accountable to God. Headship isn't a choice but an appointed responsibility.

For a more detailed analysis of this topic, consider getting the book Before You Say I Do 21 Considerations to Ponder Before Constructing a Marriage.

Reflect Now That You Have Proceeded…

Circle the flag light that best describes your assessment of yourself/ partner based on the topic: **Marriage and Headship.**

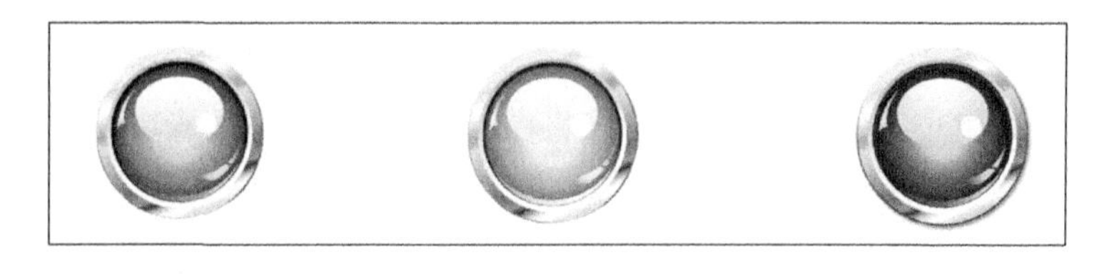

Explain your answer based your previous selection:

Know-Metre: Now appraise your knowledge of this topic after reading by circling the gauge.

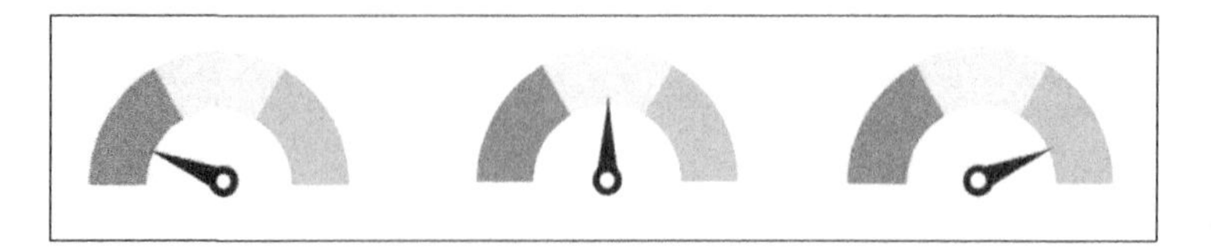

MARRIAGE AND SUBMISSION

Understanding Submission in Marriage: Navigating Roles, Mutual Respect, and Shared Decision-Making.

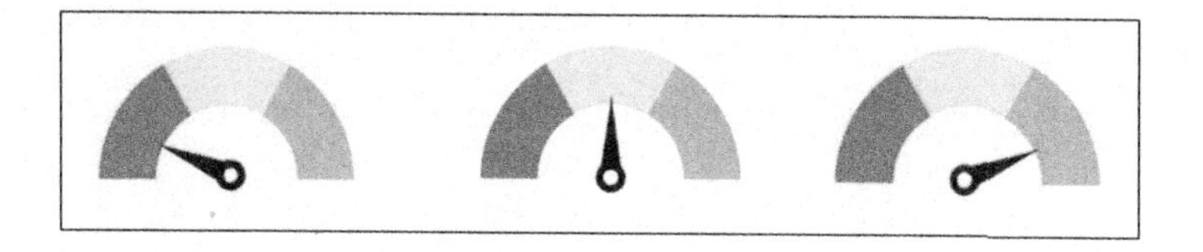

"Submission is not about authority, and it is not obedience; it is all about relationships of love and respect."

— William P. Young

The essence of "submission" lies in the amalgamation of "sub" (indicating being under) and "mission" (a significant assignment or purpose). Ephesians 5:21 emphasizes the call for mutual submission, urging individuals to "submit to each other out of reverence for Christ." This mutual submission involves aligning under the same overarching purpose, prioritising God individually and collectively.

Understanding this revealed that submission is far from a negative notion; it is actually about bestowing honour rather than losing it.

Moreover, submission adheres to a particular pattern, mirroring the relationship between Christ and the Church. Just as "Christ is the head of the church, his body, and is himself its Savior" (Ephesians 5:21). This pattern serves as a model for submission.

Ephesians 5:22-33 emphasises submission within marriage, where wives are called to submit to their husbands. This submission is not about inferiority but about a respectful response in the context of the husband's role as the head of the household, mirroring the Church's response to Christ's sacrificial love. The Greek term "hupotasso," translated as "submission," conveys the idea of supporting, ordering, or lifting rather than mere obedience. It aligns more with a voluntary act of valuing others' importance and worth equally to oneself. This original biblical concept of submission doesn't advocate for dominance or the notion of a woman completely surrendering her will to her husband, portraying him as superior. Instead, it refers to willingly serving one's partner. In Ephesians 5:22-24 MSG, the Message Translation uses 'support' instead of 'submit,' emphasising the nuanced meaning. This substitution, even though 'submit' is mentioned later in the passage, highlights the essence of the concept.

The idea of submission isn't about a woman losing her autonomy; otherwise, Paul wouldn't have expressed in 1 Corinthians 7:4 that she also has authority over her body in the relationship, indicating a mutual give-and-take. Some Bible versions note the mutual authority spouses hold over each other's bodies, accentuating a joint sense of respect that contradicts the common misconception of submission as oppressive.

In 1 Corinthians 7:4, the Message Translation underlines the essence of marriage not being a battleground for asserting one's rights but a commitment to selflessly serve each other, whether in intimacy or daily life. Marriage is a decision to serve each other, whether in bed or out! In a Christian marriage, submission is about selflessness, service, mutual accountability, and respect for one's partner. It's not about slavery or silencing a woman's voice. At its core, Christian marriage is founded on love, and love doesn't seek to control but rather to uplift, honour, and cherish.

The call to submission in marriage is mutual and not gender based. "And further, submit to one another out of reverence for Christ" (Ephesians 5:21 NLT). While the wife is called to submit to her husband's leadership, the husband is simultaneously called to love his wife sacrificially and lead the family with humility, care, and consideration for his wife's well-being. Remember, the idea of submission within a Christian marriage is intertwined with the husband's role as a servant leader. Rather than exercising authority or control, the husband is called to sacrificially love and serve his wife, mirroring Christ's love for the Church. Both partners have equal value but may have different roles within the marriage. Again, submission in this context does not diminish the wife's worth or value; it encourages her to respect and honour her husband's leadership while the husband leads with love and selflessness.

Modern interpretations of submission often align it with equality, mutual respect, and shared decision-making within a marriage. Many contemporary Christian couples understand submission as a call to honour and respect each other, recognising the value of mutual submission and sacrificial love. Therefore, submission within a Christian marriage aims to foster unity and partnership. It's about embracing humility, mutual respect, and a shared commitment to the marriage, not a one-sided or oppressive dynamic.

Dear couple,
Submission in a marriage, as understood from biblical teachings, aims to promote unity, mutual respect, and sacrificial love within the marital relationship. It's about embracing the roles of leadership and submission with the aforementioned characteristics and a commitment to the family's well-being. Embracing this principle in a

contemporary context allows couples to navigate their marital journey with mutual understanding, respect, and a shared commitment to the unity and success of the marriage.

For a more detailed analysis, consider getting the book Before You Say I Do 21 Considerations to Ponder Before Constructing a Marriage.

Reflect Now That You Have Proceeded...

Circle the flag light that best describes your assessment of yourself/ partner based on the topic: **Marriage and Submission.**

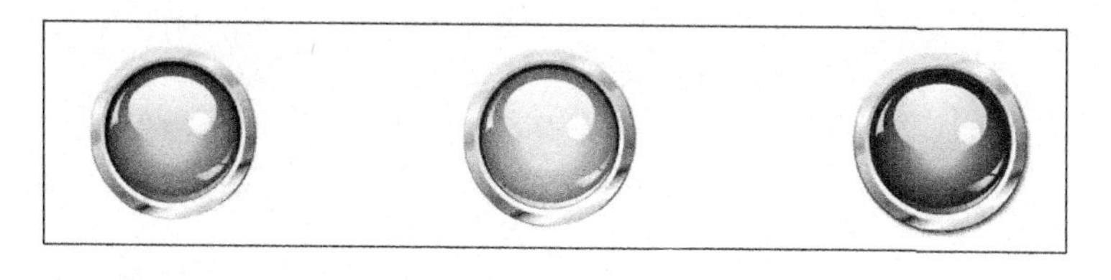

Explain your answer based your previous selection:

Know-Metre: Now appraise your knowledge of this topic after reading by circling the gauge.

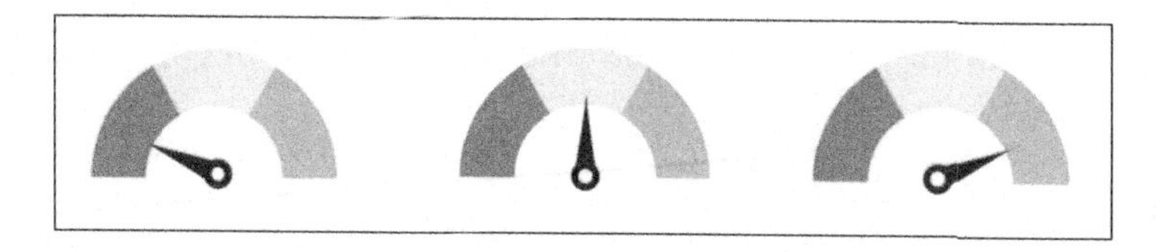

MARRIAGE AND COMMUNICATION

Fostering Connection: The Crucial Role of Effective Communication in a healthy Marriage.

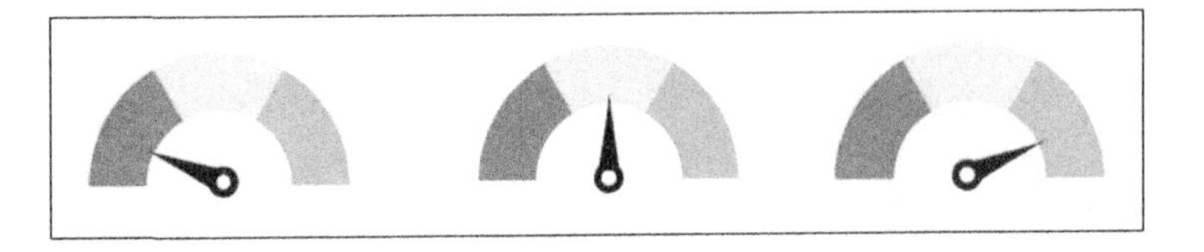

"Good communication is essential to a good and healthy marriage."
—Unknown

Communication forms the backbone of a successful and thriving marriage. It goes beyond just conveying thoughts; it's about truly understanding and being understood. It involves active listening, empathy, and openness. Partners must express themselves honestly yet respectfully, sharing both joys and concerns. This form of communication fosters an atmosphere of trust and mutual support, allowing for the resolution of conflicts with patience and understanding. It's not just about words but also about non-verbal cues, gestures, and the willingness to connect on a deeper emotional level.

When communication thrives in a marriage, it cultivates intimacy, strengthens bonds, and lays the groundwork for a resilient partnership capable of weathering life's challenges together.

Communication is the means by which couples share their thoughts, emotions, needs, and concerns. Effective communication fosters understanding, intimacy, and trust within the marriage, but couples must be open and honest. Both partners should feel comfortable expressing their thoughts and emotions without fear of judgment. This open dialogue sets the stage for better understanding and resolution of conflicts.

Active listening becomes a critical component. It involves fully engaging with your partner's words, understanding their perspective, and responding empathetically. Partners must understand each other's emotions and need to foster a deeper connection. Hence, it is critical to be very observant. Non-verbal cues such as body language, tone of voice, and facial expressions often convey more than words.

Understanding and being aware of these cues can prevent misunderstandings and improve communication.

Because conflicts are inevitable in any relationship, effective communication is crucial for resolution. It involves addressing issues respectfully, actively listening to each other's viewpoints, and working together to find a solution that benefits both partners. Establish communication patterns in your marriage. This is healthy and might involve: Setting aside dedicated time for meaningful conversations. Respecting each other's need for space. Actively engaging in both serious and light-hearted discussions.

As you navigate marriage, differences in communication styles, misunderstandings, or personal stressors may create communication challenges. Addressing these challenges requires patience, understanding, and a willingness to adapt to each other's communication needs. Together, partners must commit to continual growth and learning because effective communication is an ongoing process. Couples should continually seek to improve their communication skills, learn from past experiences, and adapt to each other's evolving needs and communication styles.

Dear couple,

Communication is the lifeblood of a successful marriage. Effective communication nurtures understanding, intimacy, and trust, creating a stronger, more resilient bond between partners. By fostering open, honest, and empathetic communication, couples can navigate challenges, resolve conflicts, and deepen their connection, enabling a fulfilling and enduring marital relationship. Remember, it's not just what is said but how it's said and received that determines the strength and vitality of a marriage. The couple should then keenly acknowledge the immense power of words. Proverbs 18:21 states, "The tongue has the power of life and death." Words possess the ability to uplift, inspire, and heal, but they also carry the potential to wound, break, and destroy. In marriage, understanding the weight of words becomes paramount. Choosing words carefully, with love and respect, nurtures the bond between partners, fostering an environment of safety and trust.

Conflict is inevitable in any relationship, but how it is managed defines the strength of the marital bond. Ephesians 4:26 guides, "Do not let the sun go down while you are still angry." Addressing conflicts promptly, with humility and a willingness to seek resolution, prevents bitterness from taking root. The act of forgiveness, as demonstrated in the biblical narrative, offers a path to healing. Colossians 3:13 advises, "Bear with each other and forgive one another if any of you has a grievance against someone. Forgive as the Lord forgave you."

God created everyone uniquely, and within marriage, these differences can be a source of strength. 1 Peter 3:7 teaches, "Husbands, in the same way, be considerate as you live with your wives and treat them with respect." Acknowledging and honouring each other's differences—be it in communication styles, preferences, or perspectives—fosters an environment of acceptance and appreciation. Embracing these distinctions allows for growth, learning, and a deeper understanding of one another.

Communication in marriage underscores the significance of seeking divine guidance. Philippians 4:6 encourages, "Do not be anxious about anything, but in every situation, by prayer and petition, with thanksgiving, present your requests to God." Couples are encouraged to pray together, seeking wisdom, patience, and strength to navigate the complexities of married life. Through prayer, spouses invite God into their relationship, finding solace and guidance in moments of joy and challenge alike.

Communication in marriage, as viewed through the lens of biblical teachings, isn't merely a tool for exchanging information but a sacred dance of love, empathy, and understanding. It requires a commitment to nurturing each other's hearts, minds, and spirits. By embracing the wisdom imparted in the scriptures, couples can weave a tapestry of communication that strengthens their marital bond, fostering a union that reflects the divine love and grace bestowed upon them.

For a more detailed analysis of this topic, consider getting the book Before You Say I Do 21 Considerations to Ponder Before Constructing a Marriage.

Reflect Now That You Have Proceeded…

Circle the flag light that best describes your assessment of yourself/ partner based on the topic: **Marriage and Communication.**

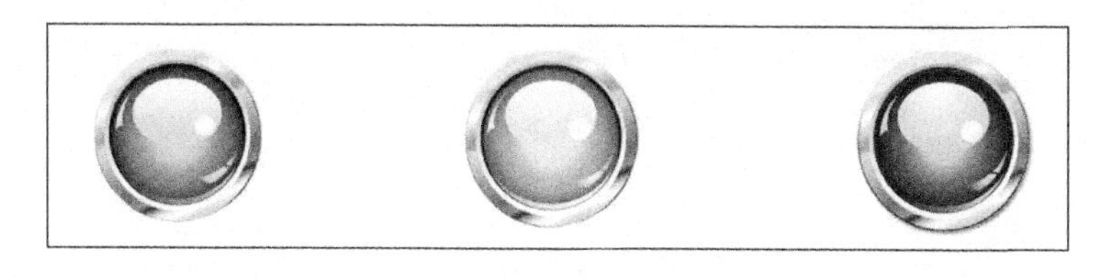

Explain your answer based your previous selection:

Know-Metre: Now appraise your knowledge of this topic after reading by circling the gauge.

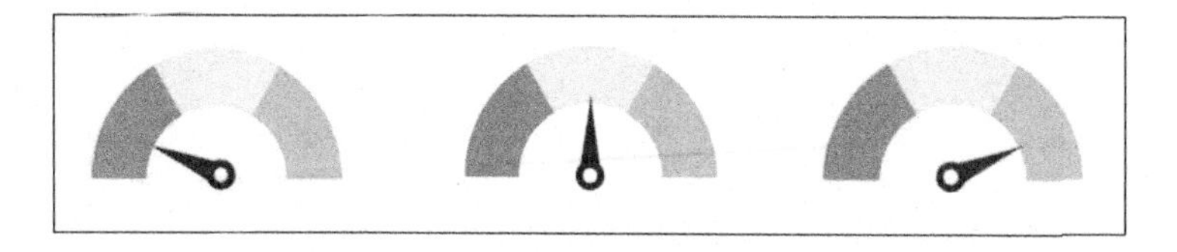

MARRIAGE AND BLENDED FAMILY

Building Harmony and Unity in Blended Marital Relationships

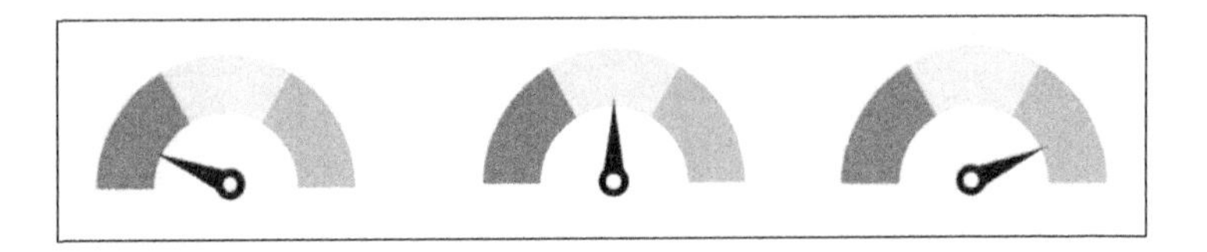

"Marriage is not a ritual or an end. It is a long, intricate, intimate dance together and nothing matters more than your own sense of balance and your choice of partner."

– Amy Bloom

Blended families bring together unique dynamics and complexities in marriage, weaving together different backgrounds, histories, and experiences. Navigating this intricate landscape requires patience, understanding, and a commitment to fostering unity. It involves not only the bond between partners but also the delicate balance of integrating children from previous relationships into a new family structure. Successful marriages in blended families often prioritize open communication, flexibility, and empathy.

Building relationships with stepchildren, respecting their emotions, and acknowledging the challenges of adjustment are crucial. It's about creating a supportive environment where everyone feels valued and heard, working together to establish new traditions and routines while honouring the individuality of each family member. Ultimately, a strong marriage in a blended family stems from love, adaptability, and a shared dedication to nurturing a harmonious and inclusive home.

A blended family, or stepfamily, takes shape when you and your partner build a life together that includes children from one or both of your previous relationships. The process of creating a new, blended family can be both fulfilling and demanding. While you, as parents, may approach remarriage and the prospect of a new family with excitement, your children or your new spouse's children may not share the same enthusiasm. They may experience uncertainty about the impending changes and how they will impact their relationships with their biological parents. There may also be concerns about living with new stepsiblings, whom they may not know well or, in some cases, may not even like.

Some children may resist these changes, and parents might become frustrated when their new family doesn't function in the same way as their previous one. Although blending families is rarely a straightforward process, the following tips can assist your new family in navigating the challenges. Regardless of how strained or difficult things may initially appear, maintaining open communication, fostering mutual respect, and offering plenty of love and patience can help you develop a close bond with your new stepchildren, eventually forming an affectionate and successful blended family. If the family succeeds, marriage will be more enjoyable.

Let us explore some tips that will help you join your family together while you are pursuing a successful marriage:

Acknowledging the complexity of blended families

Blended families merge individuals who bring their own experiences, traditions, and dynamics. Understanding and respecting these differences is vital in building a successful family unit.

Open communication and flexibility

Communication is essential in navigating the complexities of blended families. Encouraging open discussions about roles, expectations, and traditions can foster understanding and flexibility, enabling a smoother transition into the new family structure.

Creating new family dynamics

Blended families often require the creation of new family roles and structures. This might involve discussing and establishing new traditions, rules, and expectations that work for the new family unit.

Patience and understanding

Patience is key in blended families. It's essential to recognise that the process of blending takes time. Understanding each family member's unique challenges and providing support can help build a sense of security and trust.

Respect for each other's experiences

Respect for each family member's past experiences and relationships is crucial. Acknowledging and respecting each member's history and connections will help create a more inclusive and supportive environment.

Unity in parenting

It is vital to create a unified parenting approach within blended families. Couples should work together to establish consistent rules, boundaries, and discipline strategies to maintain a cohesive family environment.

Embracing flexibility and adaptability

Flexibility and adaptability are fundamental to the success of blended families. Being open to changes and adjustments in family dynamics and roles can help create a more harmonious environment.

Seeking professional guidance

In some cases, seeking the help of a family therapist or counsellor can be beneficial in navigating the complexities of blending families. Professional guidance offers support and strategies for managing conflicts and establishing a more robust family unit.

Blending families presents unique challenges, but with commitment, patience, and open communication, it is possible to build a strong, loving, and harmonious family unit. By embracing differences, creating new family dynamics, and fostering open communication, couples can navigate the complexities of blended families, creating a nurturing and supportive environment for all family members. Remember, the journey of mutual understanding, respect, and adaptability strengthens the bond of a blended family.

Dear couple,
God emphasises the importance of family, urging responsible care and support for one another. Men are encouraged to lead their families well, nurturing respectful children (1 Timothy 3:4). Women are advised to teach goodness, display modesty and submission, and guide younger women in loving their

spouses and children (Titus 2:3-5). Providing for relatives, especially those in the household, is highlighted (1 Timothy 5:8). Children are instructed to honour and obey parents if it aligns with God's will (Ephesians 6:1-3). Grown children must care for aging parents (1 Timothy 5:4). These principles apply universally to families, blended or otherwise.

Above all relationships, the connection with God holds supreme importance. The family naturally aligns when God is at the centre of a marriage. The biblical account of Adam and Eve signifies the bond in marriage, emphasising leaving one's parents to unite as one (Genesis 2:24; Matthew 19:5). A solid marital bond fosters a stronger family unit.

Blended families combine different households with varying rules, traditions, and habits. Assisting children through this transition is vital. Cooperation, patience, and communication are essential. Children need assurance and stability from both biological and stepparents. Fair and consistent disciplinary rules should be established for all children.

In stepfamilies, time division often occurs when children visit the noncustodial parent. Fostering a positive relationship with the other parent and aligning strategies for discipline and household rules, if feasible, is recommended. A structured and predictable household is beneficial. Like Jesus relying on Joseph, mutual support and recognising the need for companionship and solitude (Matthew 26:38), are crucial. Encouragement, positive role modelling, and integrity rooted in spiritual guidance should characterise family interactions.

Reflect Now That You Have Proceeded...

Circle the flag light that best describes your assessment of yourself/ partner based on the topic: **Marriage and Blended Family.**

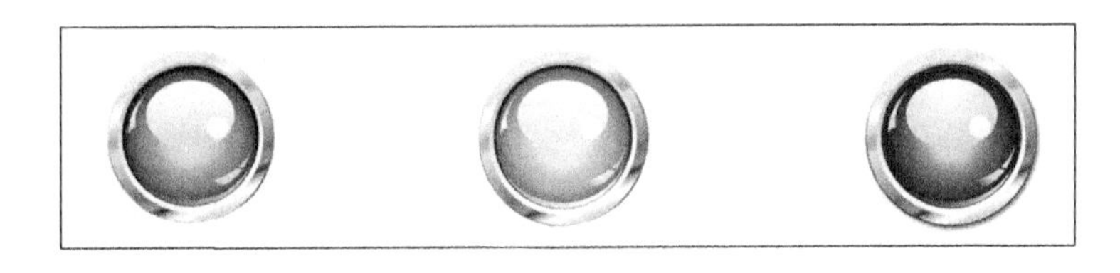

Explain your answer based your previous selection:

Know-Metre: Now appraise your knowledge of this topic after reading by circling the gauge.

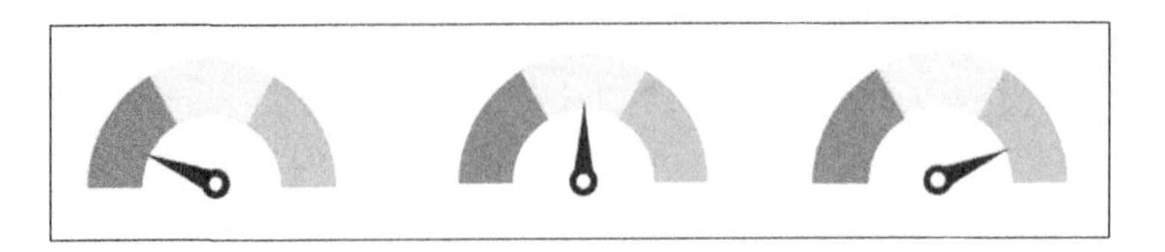

MARRIAGE AND DIVERSE VIEWS

Navigating Cultural, Religious, and Political Diversity in Marriage

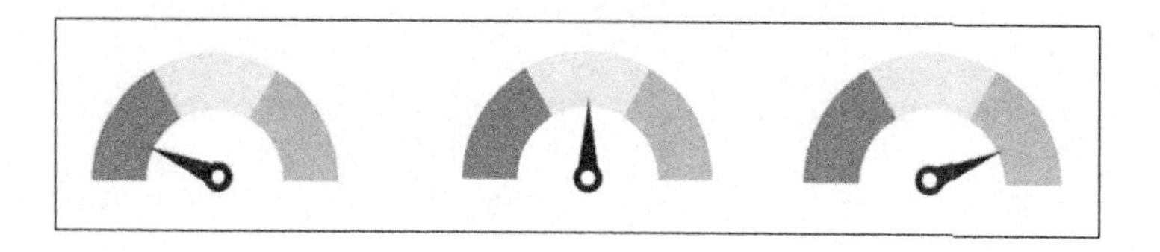

"A happy marriage doesn't mean you have a perfect spouse or a perfect marriage. It simply means you've chosen to look beyond the imperfections in both." — Fawn Weaver

Marriage can be a beautiful union that thrives on the diversity of perspectives brought in by each spouse. Sometimes, these differing views can spark vibrant discussions, offering a broader spectrum of ideas and approaches to various aspects of life. While it's natural for partners to have contrasting opinions on matters such as finances, parenting, or even personal beliefs, the strength of a marriage often lies in the ability to navigate these differences with mutual respect and understanding. It calls for open-mindedness, a willingness to listen, and the capacity to find common ground, even amidst divergent viewpoints. Embracing these distinctions can enrich the relationship, allowing each partner to learn from the other and encouraging a deeper appreciation for the uniqueness they each bring to the marriage. The key often lies not in complete agreement but in the art of respectful dialogue and common ground, fostering a space where both spouses feel heard and valued.

In the intricate fabric of marriage, the threads of cultural, religious, and political diversity weave a tapestry that, when celebrated, brings richness and depth to the relationship. A vibrant and inclusive marriage is cultivated by acknowledging and celebrating the diverse cultural, religious, and political perspectives that each partner brings into the union. This celebration becomes the foundation for a relationship that thrives on the uniqueness woven by two individuals.

Effective communication serves as the compass guiding couples through the complexities of diverse backgrounds. Engaging in open and respectful discussions about cultural, religious, and political disparities fosters understanding and empathy, building bridges over potential divides. Fundamental to harmony is the recognition and respect for each other's differences. The act of honouring customs and beliefs creates an atmosphere of inclusivity within the marriage, strengthening the bond between partners.

Couples can discover unity in shared values, principles, or goals. Identifying common ground becomes a pivotal step in establishing a cohesive marital foundation that transcends diversity. Navigating the intricate dance of diversity requires flexibility. Being open to blending traditions and accommodating each other's practices will foster an environment where both partners can coexist harmoniously.

Raising children in a culturally, religiously, or politically diverse household requires a delicate balance. Open dialogue and compromise become essential in parenting decisions, allowing the family to embrace the richness of each background. Of a truth, differing views may present challenges, but tackling them as a united front strengthens the bond. Understanding and navigating challenges as a team will contribute to the resilience and unity that define a robust relationship.

In moments of conflict arising from diversity, seeking guidance from cultural or religious advisors becomes a valuable resource. Professional support offers strategies for understanding and navigating diverse backgrounds, reinforcing the foundation of the marital union.

Dear couple,
Cultural, religious, and political differences are the brushstrokes that paint the canvas of your shared journey. Embrace these diversities with open hearts, mutual respect, and a commitment to learning from one another. In this way, your marriage becomes not only a celebration of diversity but a testament to the strength of understanding, respect, and shared commitment.

Reflect Now That You Have Proceeded...

Circle the flag light that best describes your assessment of yourself/ partner based on the topic: **Marriage and Navigating Diverse Views**

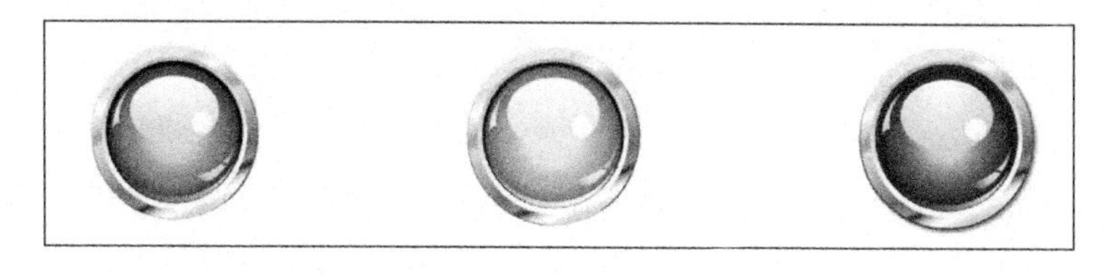

Explain your answer based your previous selection:

Know-Metre: Now appraise your knowledge of this topic after reading by circling the gauge.

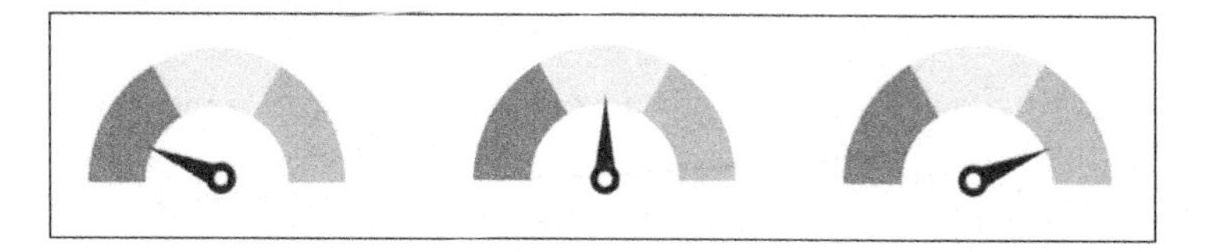

MARRIAGE AND EXTERNAL RELATIONSHIPS

Balancing Social Connections and Marital Harmony

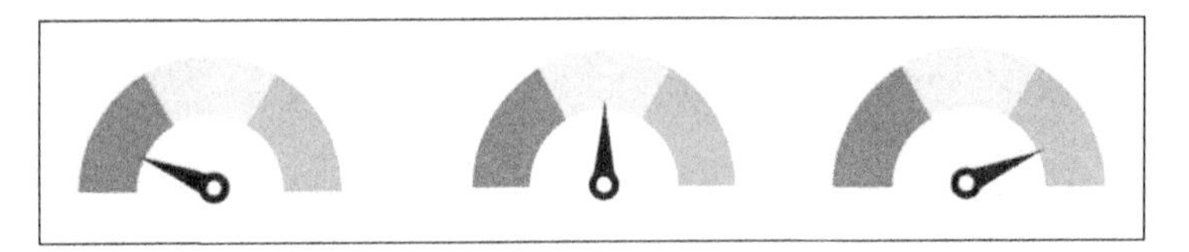

"In marriage, our love is a fortress, protecting the sacred bond from external storms, and our commitment shields us as we navigate the world hand in hand." — Unknown

Friendship outside of marriage is an invaluable facet of life, providing a unique space for camaraderie, support, and understanding. These friendships often offer perspectives and connections that complement the intimacy within a marriage. They allow for an exchange of thoughts, experiences, and emotions that might differ from those shared with their partner. These friendships thrive on mutual respect, trust, and a genuine desire to uplift one another, contributing to personal growth and emotional fulfilment. When nurtured respectfully, these connections can enhance and strengthen the foundation of marriage by fostering individual happiness and a broader network of support and companionship.

External friendships are essential for personal growth, support, and social interaction. They offer avenues for companionship, shared interests, and emotional support outside the marital relationship. Having friends to confide in and seek advice or encouragement from can alleviate stress and enhance one's mental health. Apart from the marital relationship, external friendships help maintain individual identity and allow for personal growth and fulfilment in various aspects of life. It is crucial, however, that you are also conscious that too much time spent with friends or family reduces the amount of time available to spend with your spouse. We recommend the following considerations for maintaining a healthy balance between social connections and marriage:

Mutual respect and boundaries

Maintaining friendships outside the marriage requires mutual respect and setting boundaries. It's essential to ensure that these friendships don't compromise the integrity or trust within the marital relationship.

Open communication with spouse

Open and transparent communication with your spouse about external friendships is crucial. Discussing the nature of friendships, boundaries, and any concerns helps in fostering trust and understanding.

Balancing time and priorities

Balancing time between external friendships and the marriage is essential. Prioritizing quality time with the spouse while also nurturing external friendships ensures a healthy balance.

Common friends and social circles

Having common friends or shared social circles can positively impact the marital relationship. Building friendships together helps in strengthening the bond and fostering a sense of community. Couples often bring together their individual groups of friends through marriage, creating a collective circle referred to as "our friends." Despite the strong bonds with other couples, it's probable that you have single friends or those who prefer one-on-one interactions rather than joining you as a couple, in which case we encourage you to discuss any relationship with your partner.

Respecting the spouse's comfort level

Respecting the spouse's comfort level with external friendships is vital. If there are concerns or discomfort, it's important to address them and find a common place that ensures both partners feel secure and respected.

Dear couple,

External friendships can significantly contribute to your individual life and well-being. They offer support, shared experiences, and personal growth. Nurturing these friendships while maintaining a healthy, respectful, and balanced connection within your union is paramount. Remember, its open communication, mutual respect, and the ability to find a balance that ensures external friendships enhance rather than detract from the marital relationship.

Reflect Now That You Have Proceeded...

Circle the flag light that best describes your assessment of yourself/ partner based on the topic: **Marriage and External Relationships.**

Explain your answer based your previous selection:

Know-Metre: Now appraise your knowledge of this topic after reading by circling the gauge.

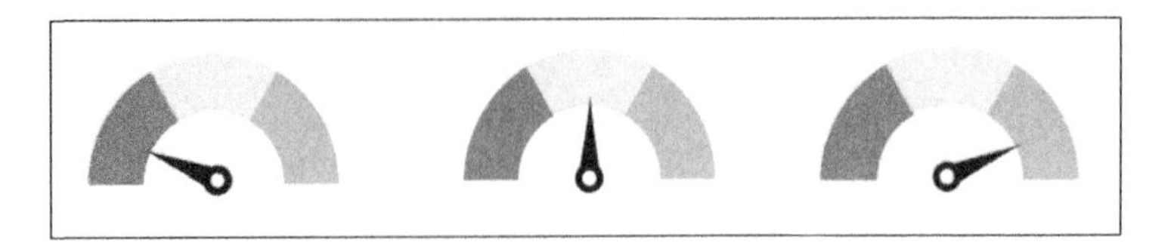

MARRIAGE AND TRAUMA

Navigating the Impact of Trauma on Marriage

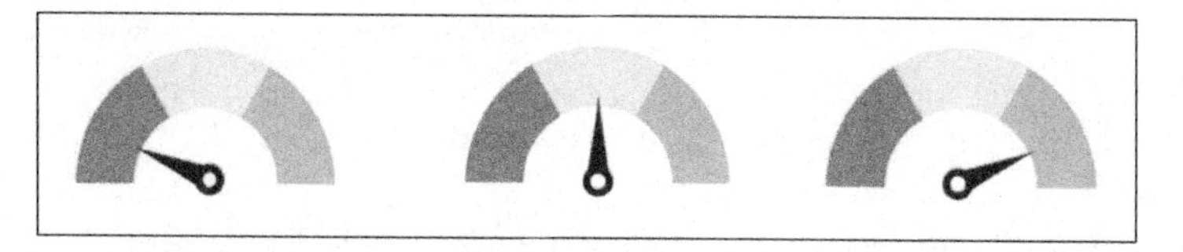

"True love is inexhaustible. The more you give, the more you have." — Antoine De Saint-Exupery

Navigating trauma within a marriage requires immense compassion, patience, and open communication. Trauma can significantly impact both partners, altering dynamics and triggering emotional challenges. Creating a safe space where both individuals feel heard and supported without judgment is crucial. Couples often find solace in seeking professional guidance through therapy or counselling to learn effective coping mechanisms and strengthen their bond. Patience becomes a guiding light as healing from trauma is a nonlinear journey; understanding that each person copes differently and offering unwavering support is essential.

Honesty, empathy, and a willingness to actively listen to each other's needs are the pillars to rebuild trust and resilience within the marriage. The process, although arduous, can deepen the emotional connection between partners, fostering a stronger, more resilient union built on mutual understanding and support. Experiencing trauma can profoundly affect individuals and their relationships.

Relationship trauma can stem from various sources like infidelity, abuse, neglect, or a significant traumatic incident. This type of trauma typically results in emotions like pain, confusion, and mistrust. Additionally, it often contributes to issues such as impaired communication, fractured trust, and unhealthy relationship patterns. It can also instigate enduring feelings of hurt, betrayal, and fear that persist continually.

Identifying the impact of trauma in marriage can be challenging, as its effects may not manifest immediately; however, this is crucial for the couple to build a thriving marriage. Let us explore some of the effects trauma has on marriage:

- **Communication challenges**

Experiencing trauma can disrupt healthy communication in relationships. The impact of trauma on the brain and body may result in the inability to articulate thoughts, leading to emotional outbursts instead of effective emotional communication. This dynamic can foster misunderstandings and create emotional distance between partners.

- **Trust issues**

Trauma, whether external or within the relationship, can hinder the establishment of trust. Trust issues often manifest as jealousy, suspicion, or a constant need for reassurance. Building a close connection with a partner becomes challenging when trust is compromised.

- **Emotional distancing**

Couples may become emotionally distant as they process their traumatic experiences. The pervasive sense that one cannot rely on anyone, including their partner, contributes to feelings of being a burden or the belief that they should handle things independently. This emotional disconnection results in simultaneous feelings of loneliness and isolation for both partners.

- **Challenges in intimacy**

Trauma frequently affects emotional and physical intimacy. The vulnerability required for intimacy can feel unsafe and out of control for those who have experienced trauma. The forced vulnerability during traumatic events may impact the reciprocity essential for emotional and physical intimacy, potentially straining sexual and emotional closeness.

- **Flashbacks and triggers in relationships**

Unresolved trauma can resurface within relationships, manifesting as visual, emotional, or physical remnants triggered by behaviours, needs, fears, or interactions. These flashbacks and triggers, though not always directly related to the trauma, significantly impact the relationship, causing distress, confusion, concern, frustration, and isolation.

- **Anger and irritability**

Trauma can manifest as anger and irritability due to its impact on the brain's emotion regulation centres. Survivors may experience bursts of outrage and anger, creating a hostile environment within the marriage because of unresolved trauma.

- **Avoidance behaviour**

Some individuals coping with trauma may develop avoidance behaviour, withdrawing from themselves, their partners, traumatic memories, and even conversations or situations that trigger trauma. This flight response can lead to marital disconnection and feelings of abandonment by the other spouse.

- **Self-Esteem challenges caused**

Trauma can detrimentally affect self-esteem and self-worth, influencing how individuals perceive themselves within the marriage and how they believe their partner sees them. Negative beliefs about oneself or the world can arise, impacting their emotional and physical well-being.

- **Disruption of roles within marriage**

Trauma can disrupt the power dynamic within a marriage, leading to role changes where one partner may over-function while the other under-functions. The traumatized partner may take on more responsibilities, struggle to trust their spouse and manage the relationship's duties based on hypervigilance and fawning. This imbalance can result in relationship burnout and resentment.

- **Impact on parenting**

Trauma can spill over into parenting, affecting how couples raise their children. Unresolved trauma may lead to inconsistent parenting and differing approaches to discipline, causing couples to project their traumatic experiences onto their children. This can negatively impact connection, attunement, and sensitivity toward children and spouses. Navigating trauma together as a couple can be an overwhelming experience. In 2022, I returned home to the most joyous news any husband could hope for—my wife was expecting our third child. Filled with excitement, we eagerly began planning for our family's newest addition. However, our joy was abruptly shattered when my wife experienced a miscarriage. This was an incredibly challenging time for both of us. The pain was intense, and our days seemed endless. We often found ourselves in tears once the kids were off to school. Despite the difficulty, we knew we had to persevere through this moment. The resilience of our marriage, family, ministry, and plans depended on our ability to withstand the impact of this trauma.

How to cope with trauma

Coping with trauma is a complex journey, and there is no one-size-fits-all solution. However, we have compiled nine proven steps for couples to consider as they navigate this challenging path together.

Recognising the indicators of trauma

Trauma, whether from personal experiences, loss, or external events, can significantly affect individuals and their relationships. Acknowledging the impact of trauma is the first step in understanding its effects on the marriage. How is this deep feeling of emotional hurt affecting you and your relationship? Traumatic relationships can significantly affect an individual's mental, emotional, and physical well-being. Recognising the signs of trauma is crucial for seeking assistance and initiating the healing process.

Here are five indications that may suggest you are grappling with trauma following a toxic relationship:

- ***Intrusive thoughts and memories***

Among the prevalent indicators of trauma are intrusive thoughts and memories. These may manifest as flashbacks, nightmares, and unwelcome thoughts or images associated with the traumatic experience. Emotions such as fear, shame, guilt, worry, and sadness linked to the past relationship may also be present.

- ***Poor concentration and memory***

Trauma can disrupt concentration and memory, leading to difficulty focusing on tasks, difficulty retaining information, and difficulties with short-term memory.

- ***Detachment and avoidance***

Individuals who have undergone a traumatic relationship often feel a sense of detachment. They may steer clear of people, places, or activities reminiscent of the past trauma, fostering emotions of isolation, depression, and anxiety.

- ***Hyperarousal***

Those who have experienced trauma may undergo hyperarousal, marked by a perpetual sense of being on edge, heightened startle responses, and increased susceptibility to being startled. Hyperarousal can result in sleep disturbances, irritability, and difficulties in concentration.

- ***Changes in eating and sleeping habits***

Trauma can alter eating and sleeping patterns, such as sudden increases or decreases in appetite, insomnia, and challenges in falling asleep.

Managing trauma responsibly

Here are some tips for dealing with trauma as a couple:

- **Open and supportive communication**

Creating an environment of open, supportive communication is crucial when a partner is dealing with trauma. Encouraging honest conversations and active listening helps understand and support the affected partner.

- **Empathy and understanding**

Showing empathy and understanding is vital when a partner is dealing with trauma. Empathising with their emotions and experiences helps validate their feelings and foster a sense of support and comfort.

- **Seeking professional help**

In cases of severe trauma, seeking professional help through therapy or counselling is beneficial. Professional guidance offers support and strategies for coping with trauma and its impact on the marriage.

- **Patience and adaptability**

Dealing with trauma requires patience and adaptability within the marriage. Understanding that healing takes time and being flexible in accommodating the affected partner's needs is essential.

Self-care for both partners

Supporting a partner through trauma can be emotionally demanding. Both partners must prioritise self-care to maintain their mental and emotional well-being. This allows for a more robust support system within the marriage.

- **Fostering resilience and healing**

Encouraging activities that foster resilience and healing, such as meditation, exercise, or creative outlets, can aid in the healing process for the partner dealing with trauma.

- **Strengthening the marital bond**

Going through trauma together can strengthen the marital bond. Working as a team to support and understand each other fosters a deeper connection and a sense of shared resilience.

Prayer

Marriage originates from God's design, not a human creation. The union of a couple is a divine creation, and God, being the creator, possesses the utmost wisdom in fostering peace and harmony within the marriage. Researchers have concluded that prayer exerts a gravitational force on the dynamics of a marital relationship, yielding favourable outcomes such as forgiveness, trust, unity, reduced infidelity, heightened relationship satisfaction, and commitment. This positive impact is particularly pronounced when couples engage in intercessory prayer for each other. Our investigation suggests that prayer may foster increased awareness of the consequences of one's actions on a spouse, a reduction in negative emotions, and a shift towards a divine perspective, diminishing anger and frustration. Additionally, prayer serves as a self-soothing and de-escalation practice, improving couples' conflict resolution. Furthermore, prayer is linked to heightened intimacy, commitment, and communication, enriching the overall quality of the marital relationship.

Dear couple,

Dealing with trauma within a marriage is a challenging journey that requires patience, understanding, and support. Couples can navigate the impact of trauma on their relationship by fostering open communication and empathy and seeking professional guidance. Remember, the shared commitment to understanding, supporting, and healing fortifies the marital bond and promotes resilience in the face of trauma. Finally, admit your pain and disappointment to God through prayer and ask for wisdom to shift perspective and forgive.

Reflect Now That You Have Proceeded...

Circle the flag light that best describes your assessment of yourself/ partner based on the topic: **Marriage and Trauma.**

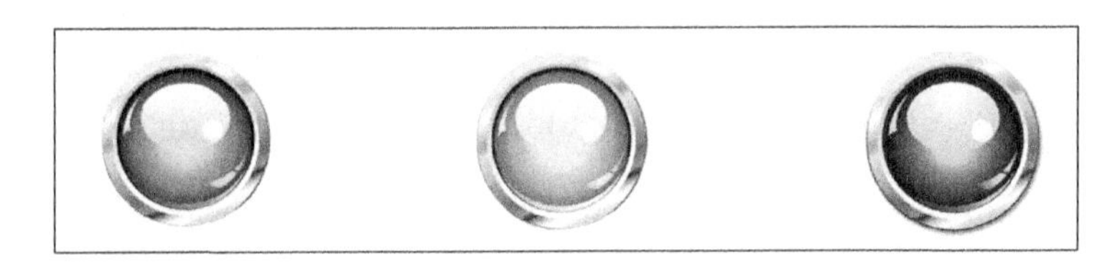

Explain your answer based your previous selection:

Know-Metre: Now appraise your knowledge of this topic after reading by circling the gauge.

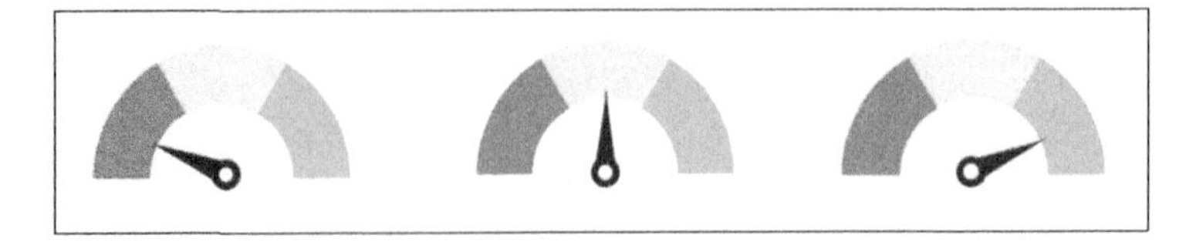

MARRIAGE AND SICKNESS

Journeying Together Through Sickness in Marital Relationships.

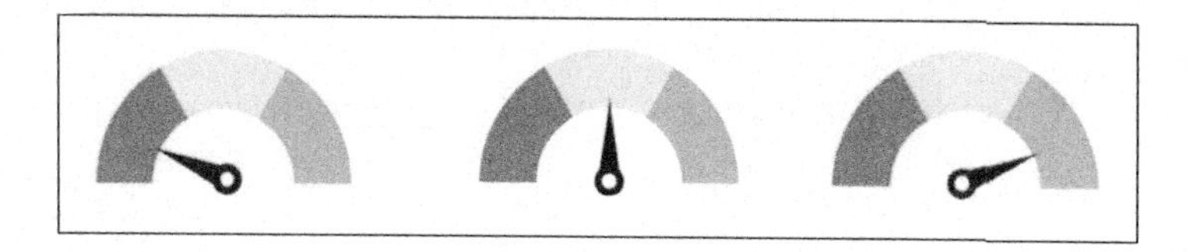

"Marriage is not just the union of two souls; it's the foundation upon which a family grows, and parenting becomes the shared masterpiece of love and commitment."

—Unknown.

Supporting each other through sickness in marriage is a testament to the unwavering bond of love and commitment. Illness can be a trying time, but within a marriage, it becomes an opportunity to showcase compassion, empathy, and care. It's a time when roles may shift, and the healthy partner steps into a nurturing role, providing not just physical aid but also emotional support. Patience and understanding will become the guiding principles, allowing the sick partner the space to heal while feeling emotionally fortified by the steadfast support of their spouse. Simple acts of kindness, like offering comfort, being a pillar of strength, and ensuring practical needs are met, strengthen the relationship's fabric. Ultimately, going through sickness together in a marriage solidifies the notion of "in sickness and in health," fostering a deeper level of trust, gratitude, and love between partners.

In one of our weekly couple's corner sessions, we listened in awe to the profound testimony of "The Broms". Mrs Brom shared her challenges with illnesses but simultaneously boasted about the support, care, and empathy of her husband. She reasoned, "Marriages can face profound challenges when one spouse falls ill or becomes disabled, requiring the other to shoulder new responsibilities. In such circumstances, it becomes necessary to redefine the expectations within the relationship. The longer the marriage, the more challenging this adjustment tends to be. Compared to adult children caring for their parents, spouses often find themselves undertaking a greater range of tasks and shouldering increased physical and financial burdens as caregivers. This increased responsibility can lead to symptoms of depression and place additional strain on the relationship. Effective communication becomes a hurdle, with both husband and wife feeling disoriented and uncertain about navigating their altered roles. There is a significant risk that marriages may be eroded by the impact of illness, leading to the loss of essential emotional connections. The well-spouse can transform profoundly from a partner and lover to a nurse and caregiver. This shift represents an entirely different dynamic within the relationship, posing challenges that need careful consideration and adaptation. With that, here are some ways a marriage can thrive through moments of adversity, explained Mrs Brom:

- **Acknowledging the impact of illness**

The onset of sickness can bring about emotional, physical, and financial challenges within a marriage. Acknowledging the impact of illness on both partners is the first step in understanding its effects on the relationship.

- **Open and empathetic communication**

Open and empathetic communication is vital when a partner is dealing with illness. Sharing feelings, concerns, and uncertainties helps build a supportive and understanding environment within the marriage.

- **Providing support and understanding**

Offering consistent and unwavering support is essential when a partner is sick. Understanding their physical and emotional needs and being a source of comfort helps navigate the challenges together.

- **Sharing responsibilities and care**

Sharing responsibilities and caregiving duties is important when a partner is sick. Both partners should contribute to the best of their abilities, creating a sense of shared commitment and mutual support.

- **Seeking professional help and information**

In situations of serious illness, seeking professional medical advice is crucial. Educating yourself about the illness and available support systems will help the well-partner cope and plan for the future.

Balancing emotional well-being

Dealing with illness can take an emotional toll on both partners. It's essential to find ways to maintain emotional well-being, possibly through support groups, therapy, or self-care practices.

Flexibility and adaptability

Flexibility and adaptability are key in dealing with sickness within a marriage. Being adaptable to changes in routines or lifestyle due to illness helps in maintaining a supportive and comfortable environment.

Fostering resilience and hope

Encouraging hope and fostering resilience within the marriage is essential. Finding moments of joy and optimism amid illness helps maintain a positive outlook.

Dear couple,

Dealing with sickness within a marriage is a challenging journey that requires compassion, support, and understanding. By fostering open communication, providing unwavering support, and seeking information and professional help, couples can navigate the impact of illness on their relationship. Remember, it's the shared commitment to understanding, supporting, and healing together that fortifies the marital bond and fosters resilience in the face of sickness.

Reflect Now That You Have Proceeded...

Circle the flag light that best describes your assessment of yourself/ partner based on the topic: **Marriage and Navigating Sickness.**

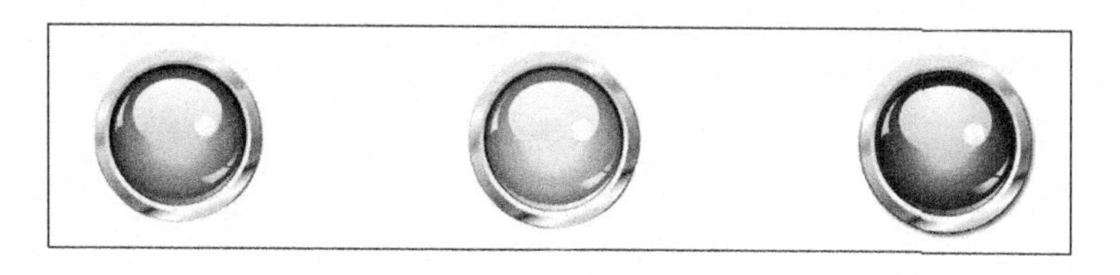

Explain your answer based your previous selection:

Know-Metre: Now appraise your knowledge of this topic after reading by circling the gauge.

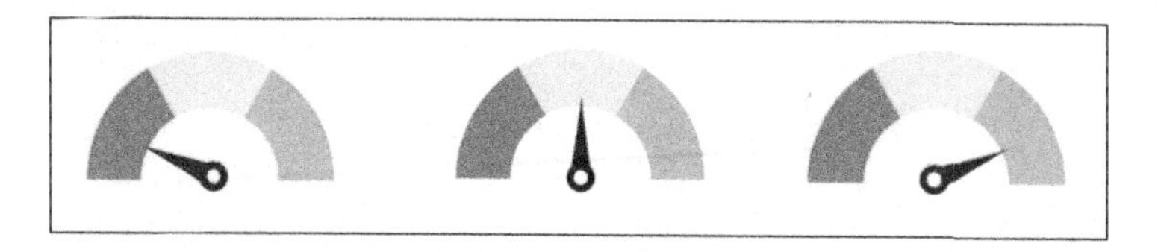

MARRIAGE AND FRIENDSHIP

The Foundation of Lasting Marital Relationships

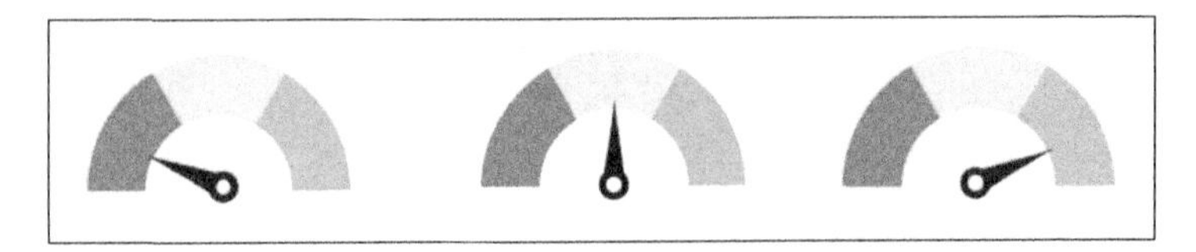

"It is not a lack of love, but a lack of friendship that makes unhappy marriages." — Friedrich Nietzsche

Friendship is a fundamental pillar of a successful and enduring marital relationship. Cultivating friendship within a marriage lays the foundation for a resilient, joy-filled partnership. It involves an intentional effort to connect beyond the roles of spouses, delving into the realms of companionship, understanding, and shared experiences. Building friendship means fostering open communication, actively listening to each other, and taking genuine interest in each other's thoughts, dreams, and daily lives. It's about finding moments of laughter, embarking on adventures together, and creating a safe space where both partners can be their authentic selves without fear of judgment.

Friendship in marriage means being each other's confidants, supporting individual growth, and celebrating the uniqueness of one another. When friendship thrives, it infuses the relationship with a deep sense of camaraderie, trust, and an enduring bond that weathers the ups and downs of life's journey together.

Friendship in marriage provides a foundation of companionship and trust. It involves sharing interests, emotions, and experiences, fostering open communication marked by transparency and honesty. This bond goes beyond mere association, deepening the connection between partners. Friends offer crucial emotional support, empathy, and a sense of security. The shared interests and enjoyable moments typical of friendships contribute to creating a fulfilling and enduring marital relationship. Allocating quality time for shared activities and respecting each other's individuality becomes pivotal in nurturing this unique friendship within the marriage.

Strengthening this friendship involves continuous efforts, such as supporting and encouraging each other and building a foundation of trust through shared accomplishments. True friends accept each other as they are, recognizing and embracing flaws and strengths. During challenging times, friendship in marriage becomes a beacon, providing support and unity. Open communication and collaborative problem-solving skills, inherent in friendships, are crucial in addressing issues within the marital relationship, fostering understanding and resolution. Together, these elements form a resilient framework for a marriage enriched by the enduring qualities of a true friend.

Communication and problem-solving, essential skills in friendship, are equally vital in marriage. Open communication and collaborative problem-solving contribute to addressing issues, fostering understanding, and finding resolutions within the marital relationship. Amidst the global pandemic in 2020, my wife and I made a significant move to the United Kingdom for a new job opportunity. Finding ourselves in a foreign land with no friends or family nearby and constrained by movement restrictions, we became each other's primary support. It was a unique phase in our marriage where, for the first time, there were no external connections to visit or speak with. This period stands out as a time when we deepened our friendship, focusing on being loving and patient with each other.

The foundation of happy marriages lies in deep friendship. A robust marriage is fundamentally rooted in high-quality friendship. The presence of such a friendship tends to correlate with elevated levels of romantic and physical satisfaction. Genuine friendship fosters anticipation for shared time and enriches life experiences through a profound emotional connection between partners.

While common interests are often touted as crucial for marital stability, the true significance lies in how these shared pursuits bring a couple together. It's not merely about having similar interests; the key factor is the relational dynamic while engaging in those interests together.

Regardless of the duration of a marriage, whether it's six months or sixty years, it's the seemingly small, everyday moments of connection that hold significant value. These subtle threads of connection, woven over time, become integral to the very fabric of a marriage. Actress Simone Signoret captured this essence, stating, "Chains do not hold a marriage together. It is thread, hundreds of tiny threads that sew people together through the years. That is what makes a marriage last—more than passion or even sex."

In the highs and lows of married life, it is beneficial to remind ourselves that, above all, we are friends. This friendship extends beyond moments of laughter, occasional hurt, shared fun, and common interests. At the core, it is the assurance that, when challenges arise, there is someone steadfastly supporting, someone who is there unconditionally.

Here are a few tips for improving the quality of friendship in marriage:

- show genuine interest in your partner's life events. celebrate victories together and offer support during tough times.
- avoid criticising each other in public; maintain respect.
- stand by your partner in challenging moments, reinforcing your shared commitment.
- recognise that even routine tasks, like loading the dishwasher, can serve as bonding opportunities to share your day.
- prioritise kindness in your interactions. remember important dates, such as birthdays and anniversaries.
- discover shared interests and activities, whether it's cooking, gardening, sports, or camping.
- make your partner feel special through thoughtful gestures, valuing simplicity over extravagance—such as running a bath or lighting a candle.
- pray for and encourage each other.

Dear couple,

Friendship within marriage forms the bedrock of a strong and enduring connection. By fostering companionship, trust, open communication, and shared experiences, couples can build a profound and lasting bond. Remember, the shared commitment to being friends, understanding, supporting, and enjoying each other's company fortifies the marital relationship, creating a resilient and enduring union built on trust, love, and genuine companionship.

Reflect Now That You Have Proceeded...

Circle the flag light that best describes your assessment of yourself/ partner based on the topic: **Marriage and Balancing Friendship.**

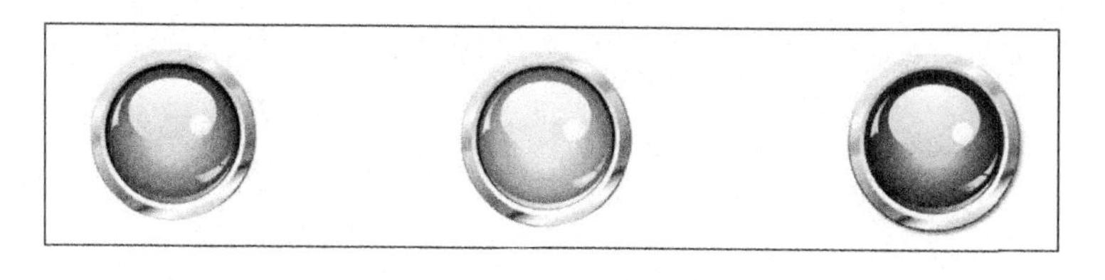

Explain your answer based your previous selection:

Know-Metre: Now appraise your knowledge of this topic after reading by circling the gauge.

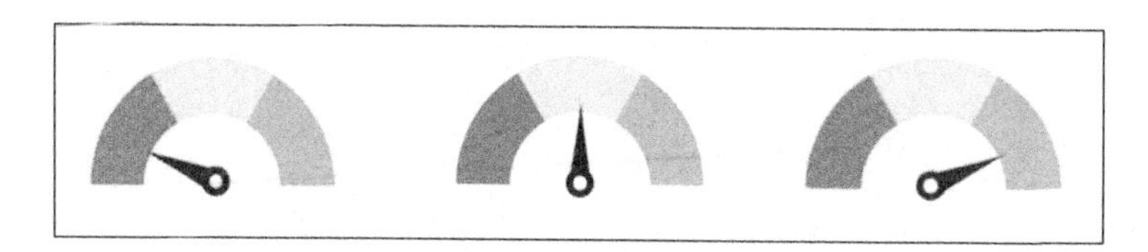

MARRIAGE, LOVE AND COMMITMENT

Nurturing Lasting Bonds Through Commitment

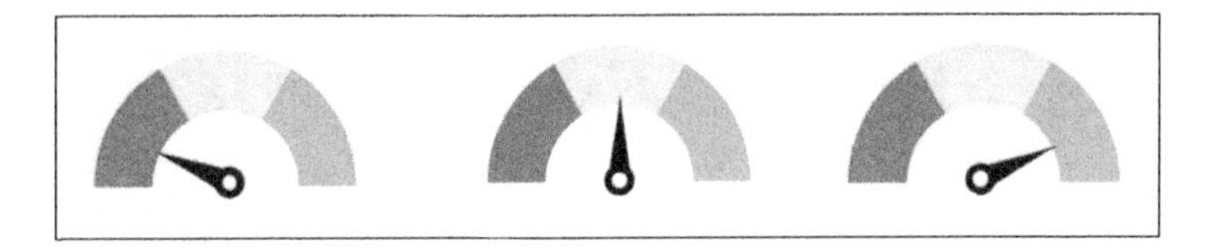

"Coming together is a beginning; keeping together is progress; working together is success." — Henry Ford

Love and commitment in marriage weave together a tapestry of trust, dedication, and unwavering support. Love in marriage encompasses both passion and deep companionship, an enduring flame that evolves through time. It involves not just romantic gestures but also the small acts of kindness, understanding, and respect shared daily. Commitment, on the other hand, is the steadfast promise to weather storms together, embrace each other's flaws, and continually choose to nurture the relationship. It's the dedication to prioritize the partnership, to communicate openly, and to navigate challenges as a united front. Love and commitment in marriage are a beautiful blend of emotions and actions, fostering an unbreakable bond that grows stronger with every passing day, transcending hurdles, and enriching the journey shared by two souls intertwined.

Commitment in marriage signifies a profound dedication to the relationship. It encompasses loyalty, fidelity, and a promise to work through challenges. As in other meaningful human interactions, commitment plays a crucial role in a successful marriage. It serves as the bedrock upon which trust, love, and mutual respect can thrive. With commitment, a marriage becomes resilient and able to withstand the substantial challenges that life presents. Marriage, essentially, is a pledge between two individuals to love and support each other for a lifetime. It involves a commitment to prioritise the needs of the partner over one's own and a dedication to navigating challenges together. "A successful marriage requires falling in love many times, always with the same person."- Mignon McLaughlin

Commitment in marriage is an indispensable factor for the success of any enduring relationship. Embracing mutual dedication is fundamental, with both partners actively contributing to the relationship, promising loyalty, support, and unwavering devotion to each other. This dedication becomes particularly evident when facing challenges together, as commitment involves standing united through adversities, be they emotional, financial, or circumstantial.

Open and honest communication is another cornerstone of commitment. Sharing feelings, thoughts, and concerns fosters understanding, nurturing a stronger, more resilient bond. Providing consistent emotional support is equally vital, as being present during challenging times and offering reassurance strengthens the very foundation of the relationship. Moreover, commitment encompasses respecting and supporting each other's individuality and acknowledging personal growth, aspirations, and differences, thereby fortifying the bond through a mutual environment of respect.

Continual effort and investment in the relationship are imperative for commitment. Regularly nurturing the emotional, physical, and mental aspects ensures a robust and lasting bond. Remaining focused on the relationship amid life's challenges reinforces commitment, prioritising the marriage amidst external demands to maintain the integrity of the bond. Forgiveness is an integral part of commitment, recognising the inevitability of human errors and offering and seeking forgiveness as needed. Finally, building trust gradually through honesty, effective communication, and a genuine willingness to be open and vulnerable with each other over time is essential, as its absence can lead to the gradual erosion of the relationship's foundation.

Dear couple,

Commitment is essential for a thriving and enduring marriage. By embracing mutual dedication, weathering challenges together, fostering open communication, and consistently supporting each other, couples can nurture a profound and lasting bond. Remember, it's the shared commitment, understanding, and unwavering support that fortifies the marital relationship, creating a resilient and enduring union built on trust, love, and devotion.

For a more detailed analysis of this topic, consider getting the book Before You Say I Do 21 Considerations to Ponder Before Constructing a Marriage.

Reflect Now That You Have Proceeded...

Circle the flag light that best describes your assessment of yourself/ partner based on the topic: **Marriage and Commitment.**

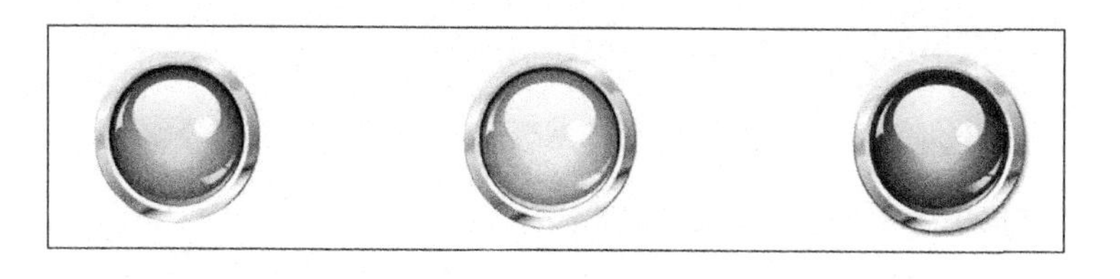

Explain your answer based your previous selection:

Know-Metre: Now appraise your knowledge of this topic after reading by circling the gauge.

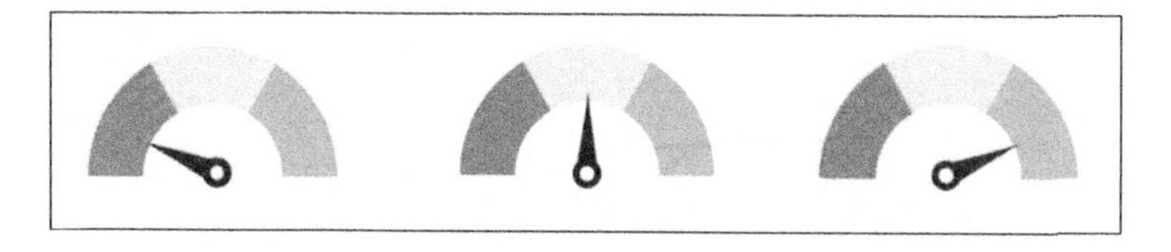

MARRIAGE AND PURITY

The Sacred Bond of Marriage and the Essence of Purity

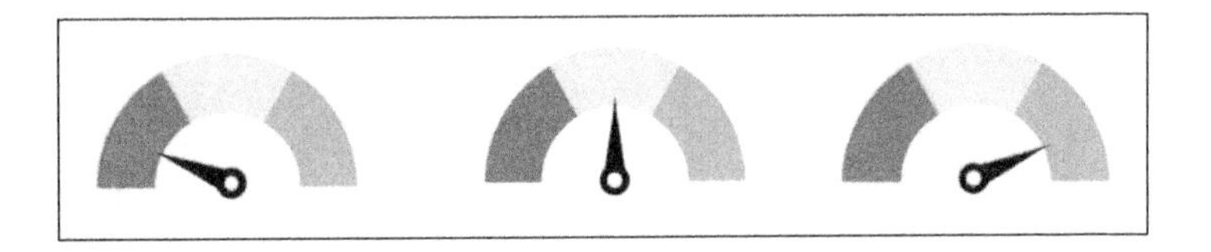

"Purity is the shared commitment to preserve the sacred bond, fostering a love that remains untarnished by the impurities of the world." — Unknown

In the fabric of human relationships, few bonds hold as much significance, depth, and sanctity as the institution of marriage. It is a union that transcends mere legal or societal recognition; it embodies a profound intertwining of hearts, minds, and souls. At the core of this union lies the concept of purity, not merely in a physical sense, but in a holistic understanding that encompasses emotional, mental, and spiritual dimensions.

Marriage, in its essence, is a covenant—a promise of companionship, support, and unwavering commitment. It provides a fertile ground for personal growth, fostering an environment where two individuals strive to nurture each other's strengths, mitigate weaknesses, and embark on a journey of shared aspirations.

Within this sacred bond, the concept of purity manifests in various forms. At its foundation lies fidelity—an unwavering loyalty and commitment to one's partner. Trust, another key component of any healthy marriage, is built through transparent communication, mutual respect, and the honouring of promises made in both subtle and grand gestures.

To foster emotional purity within marriage, couples must cultivate a safe space to express their thoughts, fears, dreams, and vulnerabilities without fear of judgment or ridicule. It's about cherishing each other's emotions, providing comfort in distress, and celebrating the joys. Understanding and empathising with your partner's feelings, listening attentively, and offering support during challenging times foster an emotional purity that forms the bedrock of a solid marital relationship.

Spiritual and mental purity

Purity in the spiritual and mental realms involves aligning shared values, beliefs, and goals. It's about nurturing each other's spiritual growth, respecting individual beliefs, and collectively finding meaning and purpose in life's journey.

Mental purity encompasses a shared intellectual connection—a space where thoughts, ideas, and perspectives are respected and explored. Encouraging intellectual growth, engaging in stimulating conversations, and fostering an environment of continuous learning are integral to mental purity in marriage.

Physical purity

Physical purity is often associated with intimacy and sexuality within the bounds of marriage. It encompasses more than just abstinence before marriage; it's about mutual respect, understanding, and the unspoken language of physical intimacy between partners. It involves honouring each other's bodies, desires, and boundaries, ensuring that physical expressions of love are a manifestation of mutual affection, trust, and consent.

Cultivating purity in marriage

Achieving and maintaining purity within the confines of marriage is an ongoing journey that demands dedication, patience, and a willingness to evolve individually and as a couple. It requires consistent efforts to communicate openly, resolve conflicts with grace and understanding, and continually nurture the love and respect that form the foundation of the marital bond.

Remember, purity in marriage is not about perfection but about the conscious effort to embrace the values of loyalty, trust, respect, and love that uphold the sanctity of this sacred union. It's an ongoing commitment to cherish, honour, and uplift each other, creating a haven of purity within the beautiful tapestry of married life.

Masturbation and purity

The Bible doesn't explicitly mention masturbation, self-gratification, or "solo sex," therefore, views on this topic vary within different Christian communities.

Some individuals believe that certain passages indirectly reference or condemn acts that might be interpreted as masturbation. For instance, the story of Onan in Genesis 38:9-10 is sometimes cited. Onan withdrew from intercourse with his deceased brother's wife, disobeying the levirate law of the time, and spilled his semen on the ground. His action was seen as disobedience and was punished by God. However, this passage is more about Onan's disobedience to God's command to fulfil his duty to his brother's widow rather than specifically addressing masturbation.

Others argue that there's no clear biblical prohibition against masturbation. They often emphasise the importance of interpreting biblical teachings within the context of the time they were written and considering broader principles of love, self-control, and purity.

Although the Bible does not directly discuss masturbation, it does delineate the purpose of sexual intimacy. Referencing 1 Corinthians 7:2–5, the passage emphasises the significance of intimate connections within marriage, indicating that sex should involve the commitment between a husband and wife. Masturbation, in contrast, exists outside this relational context.

The passage underscores the idea of giving one's body to a spouse, a key aspect of God's design for sexual intimacy. Masturbation, on the other hand, involves the containment of one's body for personal gratification. When discussing times of sexual deprivation, the solution presented is to "come together" as a couple. Masturbation, however, involves solitary activity, not shared intimacy.

First Corinthians 7:9 suggests marriage as a solution for those grappling with sexual desires. Paul stresses the importance of self-control. For individuals lacking self-restraint, the suggestion isn't to endorse masturbation but to encourage marriage as a God-sanctioned outlet for such desires.

Contrary to the belief that masturbation is a basic human need, the Bible doesn't characterise sexual fulfilment as a necessity. In fact, Paul advises the unmarried that remaining single might be preferable (1 Corinthians 7:8, NLT).

Acts commonly linked to masturbation—like entertaining lustful thoughts, inappropriate sexual arousal, or consuming pornography—are considered sinful and should be addressed. By confronting these issues, the temptation of masturbation diminishes. Many individuals grapple with guilt surrounding masturbation when, in truth, addressing the underlying sins might offer a more beneficial resolution.

The effect of masturbation on marriage

Masturbation can affect marital relationships in various ways. It's important to recognise that attitudes toward masturbation vary widely among individuals and cultures. Some individuals may see it as a natural and normal part of human sexuality, while others might have moral or religious objections to it. Others consider masturbation as a taboo or immoral, while others perceive it as a private and acceptable activity. For some couples, masturbation may impact intimacy within the relationship. It could potentially affect the frequency of sexual interactions or create emotional distance, especially if it becomes a substitute for shared intimacy. Masturbation may also provoke discomfort or misunderstandings if partners hold different views on the subject. Open and respectful communication is crucial to understanding each other's perspectives and navigating potential concerns.

Some argue that masturbation serves as a form of stress relief or self-exploration for an individual. Researchers' belief it can aid in understanding one's own body and sexual response, contributing to personal well-being. Regardless of the benefits, the act may have more negative consequences than positive. It can lead to concerns or insecurities within the relationship if one partner feels threatened or inadequate due to their partner's solo sexual activity.

Marriage was designed by God to be enjoyed by a man and a woman. Considering this, personal masturbation may be best described as a selfish act in marriage in which one person satisfies themself while depriving the other of the joyful benefit of being married. It may also highlight other problems such as unforgiveness, lack of communication, or dissatisfaction in the union, in which case, the marriage is in danger of collapse. In retrospect, it becomes uncertain whether masturbation aligns with honouring God with our bodies. To consider masturbation acceptable and pure, it would need to be devoid of:

- lustful intentions,
- threat to your partner's happiness and security,
- immoral thoughts,
- engagement with pornography,
- self-centred gratification,
- complete certainty of its righteousness,
- genuine gratitude expressed toward God.

However, these qualifiers essentially contradict the essence and intent of masturbation itself. Stripping these elements from the act seems to invalidate its purpose and significance. So, what if we use it for foreplay? There is no list outlining the specification of marital intimacy, however God doesn't disappear into the sunset when a couple partakes in sex neither does He alter His expectation. Morality is for all people. Whatever you do in marriage must honour God. Sexual intimacy strengthens marriage and foreplay is critical to fostering overwhelming showers of excitement. Foreplay creates an intense lust or desire to have sex. If done to excite the other partner within the confines of marriage, it should be regarded as pure. We are conscious that some partners may enjoy the act together. Other partners may need it as an invention where a couple is experiencing impotence and or illnesses. In this case, we do not seek to be legislators of what is deemed right or wrong. Instead, we desire to promote healthy and thriving unions. A good guiding philosophy is masturbation should not be an alternative to mutual gratification.

Dear couple,

Purity encompasses a state free from anything that taints or corrupts. It's characterised by being flawless, uncompromised, and completely unadulterated. It's about maintaining a state of wholesomeness and integrity, untouched by impurities or compromise. Masturbation's impact on marriage varies significantly based on personal beliefs, cultural backgrounds, and relationship dynamics. A healthy and understanding dialogue between partners is crucial to navigate any concerns or discomfort that might arise. Respect, communication, and mutual understanding are key to maintaining a strong and healthy marital relationship when dealing with sensitive topics such as masturbation.

Reflect Now That You Have Proceeded...

Circle the flag light that best describes your assessment of yourself/ partner based on the topic: **Marriage and Purity.**

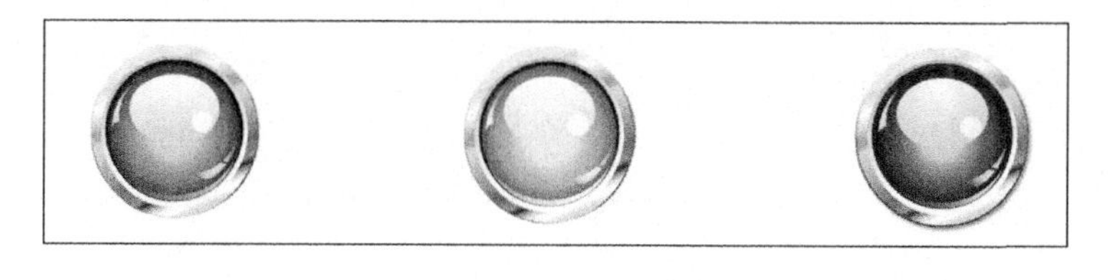

Explain your answer based your previous selection:

Know-Metre: Now appraise your knowledge of this topic after reading by circling the gauge.

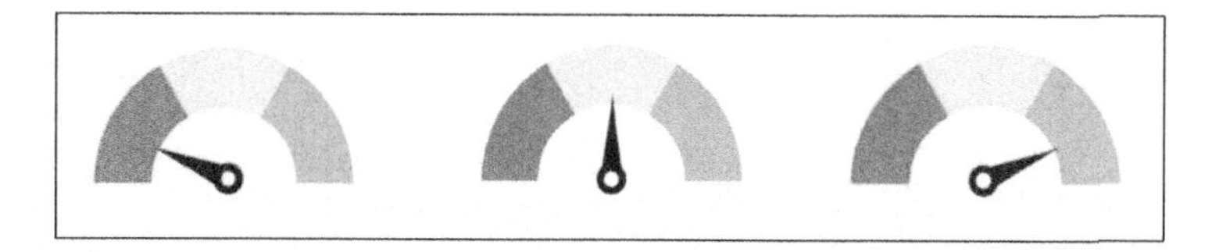

MARRIAGE AND HOLINESS

Upholding Sacred Bonds: Cultivating Holiness in Marriage by Rejecting the Intrusion of Pornography

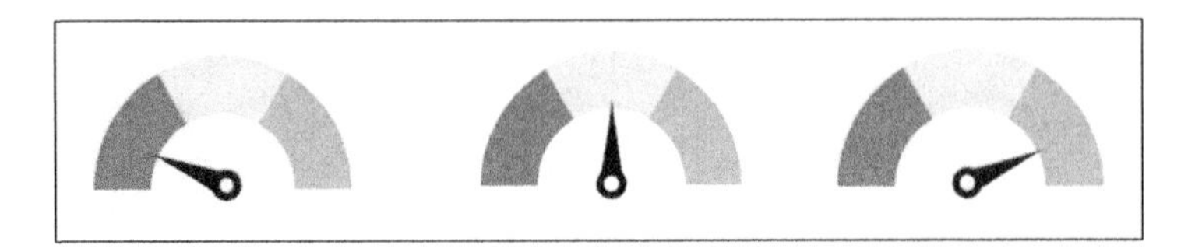

"In the sacred union of marriage, love becomes a vessel for holiness, and together, partners embark on a journey where their shared commitment transforms the ordinary into the extraordinary." — Unknown

Marriage, the sacred union between two individuals, is often viewed through cultural, societal, and religious lenses. When contemplating marriage and holiness, one delves into the profound intertwining of spiritual sanctity and the human connection within this institution.

Holiness, in its essence, signifies a state of purity, righteousness, and sacredness. It's a concept deeply rooted in religious and spiritual traditions across the world. Marriage, similarly, carries spiritual significance in many cultures, representing more than just a legal or social contract. It symbolises the union of two souls, a covenant that transcends the physical realm and touches upon the spiritual.

Marriage is a divine institution—a representation of the relationship between Christ and the Church. The sacred texts speak of the sanctity of marriage, emphasising love, fidelity, and mutual respect as foundational pillars. It is seen as a holy bond that reflects God's love and commitment.

The intertwining of marriage and holiness isn't confined solely to Christianity. Many faiths extol the virtues of marriage and its connection to spiritual growth. In Hinduism, marriage is considered a sacred duty, a pathway to fulfilling one's dharma (duty) and achieving spiritual growth through shared experiences and responsibilities.

Holiness in marriage extends beyond religious rituals and beliefs. It embodies the essence of selflessness, compassion, and unwavering support between partners. The journey toward holiness within marriage involves a continuous striving for spiritual growth and moral development as individuals and as a couple.

At its core, a holy marriage is characterised by mutual respect, understanding, and the pursuit of a shared spiritual purpose. It's a space where both partners support each other's journey toward self-discovery and spiritual fulfilment. The challenges and joys encountered in marriage become opportunities for spiritual growth, fostering qualities like patience, forgiveness, and empathy.

.

The primary goal of marriage is not for happiness. It is for holiness. The couple agrees to live faithful to each other ultimately glorifying God through marriage.

Honour marriage and guard the sacredness of sexual intimacy between wife and husband. God draws a firm line against casual and illicit sex. —Hebrews 13:4 (Message)

According to this text, the writer opines that marriage is the union of one man and one woman in wedlock, whereby they become one flesh; it is a joining together of male and female in this relation, and of two only. Marriage is instituted by God. Some have used the text to wrongfully believe that marriage means that one is at liberty to view and embrace pornography and share in other acts that defile the expectation of God, the creator of marriage. So, in this chapter, we want to answer the ensuing question:

Can couples watch pornography?

Pornography is the creation and distribution of sexually explicit material aiming to stimulate viewers and satisfy desires. The word itself originated from the Greek words "porneia" and "graphe." "Porneia" encompasses fornication, prostitution, adultery, sexual immorality, and other forms of obscenity and deviation.

Hebrews 13:4b suggests the bed of such whose marriage is honourable, which is not polluted by admitting others into it, or by acts of fornication and adultery will be judged by God. The couple engaging in the pornographic act is either guilty of fornication or adultery, making the content itself impure for viewing. Those viewing are likely to be aroused by the individuals in the video, which makes them guilty of lust.

"Graphe" is the Greek root for various methods of writing, drawing, or expression. Therefore, "pornography" refers to the depiction or description of sexually explicit content meant to sexually arouse the reader or viewer.

The term "pornography" isn't explicitly named or condemned in Scripture, which could be why this issue raises questions. However, the Bible is clear about God's expectations for His followers, particularly regarding personal and marital purity.

Therefore, watching pornography is nearly always accompanied by sexual arousal, which is its intended effect. Yet, instead of being aroused by the love and intimacy within a committed relationship, pornography stimulates through explicit images or videos of others engaging in sexual acts.

Pornography strips sex of its rightful context within marriage. It tantalises with images and thoughts, appealing to fleshly desires through the false promise of intimacy found in self-gratification rather than in a meaningful, God-honouring relationship. It prioritises personal satisfaction and instant gratification over genuine intimacy and self-discipline. Ultimately, it leads the viewer to objectify others outside the bounds of marriage.

Job expressed a commitment to purity:
"I made a covenant with my eyes not to look lustfully at a young woman. What would be the portion of God from above and the heritage of the Almighty from on high? Is it not calamity for the unjust and disaster for those who work iniquity? Does He not see my ways and number all my steps?"
– Job 31:1-4

Dr. Patrick Fagan's extensive study on pornography described it as a "quiet family killer," noting that 56% of divorces involved a partner with an obsessive interest in porn. Pornography stands as the primary temptation confronting many adult men. Left unchecked, it corrodes not only rational thinking but also the essence of one's soul. When external sexual influences infiltrate a marriage, the relationship can deteriorate, descending into despair over time.

Exceptional marital intimacy isn't solely about technique or experience; rather, it's the profound connection between two individuals deeply in love, manifesting in the highest form of physical closeness. Pornography seeks to replicate this marital passion. As a multi-billion-dollar industry, it relies on visually captivating content for success. However, real-life relationships, including sexual intimacy, differ drastically from the glossy portrayals of porn.

Consuming porn shapes unrealistic expectations that individuals carry into their intimate relationships, leading to dissatisfaction for both partners. Many wives view their husband's pornography consumption as a form of infidelity. Continuous exposure to porn gradually erodes the trust within a marriage, concurrently diminishing the ability to experience genuine intimacy.

Men ensnared by pornography often justify their actions, deflecting blame onto their partners or circumstances while attempting to mask the shame they feel. However, the fleeting gratification offered by porn fails to compare to the genuine connection experienced with a spouse. Like other addictions, pornography demands increasing doses for the same initial satisfaction, leaving individuals in perpetual pursuit of an unattainable high.

Ultimately, individuals grappling with a porn addiction face a critical juncture: seeking help or witnessing their lives unravel bit by bit due to the relentless grip of this addiction.

Dear couple,

Rejecting pornography within a marriage is a conscious commitment to prioritise genuine intimacy, trust, and respect. It's about fostering a healthy emotional and physical connection between partners rooted in mutual understanding and support. By choosing to abstain from pornography, couples affirm the importance of real, meaningful interactions that honour each other's dignity and boundaries. It opens the door to deeper communication, allowing for exploration and fulfilment in ways that reinforce the unique bond shared between spouses. This rejection isn't merely about avoiding an external influence; it's a deliberate choice to nurture a relationship built on authenticity, empathy, and a profound sense of closeness. , the intertwining of marriage and holiness illuminates the profound spiritual dimension embedded within this institution. It's a journey of self-discovery, mutual growth, and shared spiritual aspirations. When approached with reverence, respect, and a commitment to spiritual growth, marriage becomes a pathway toward experiencing and nurturing holiness in daily life.

Reflect Now That You Have Proceeded...

Circle the flag light that best describes your assessment of yourself/ partner based on the topic: **Marriage and Holiness.**

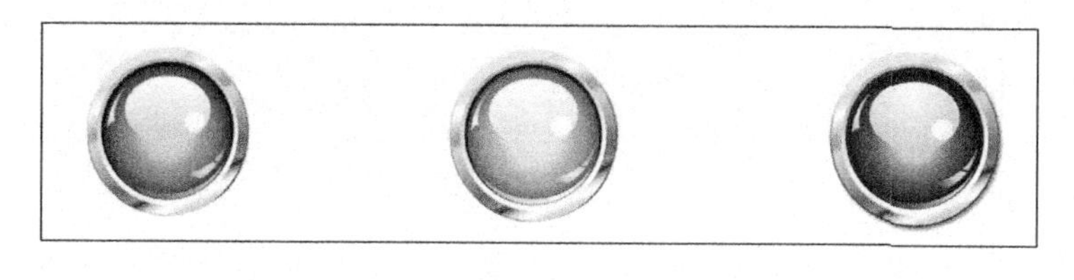

Explain your answer based your previous selection:

Know-Metre: Now appraise your knowledge of this topic after reading by circling the gauge.

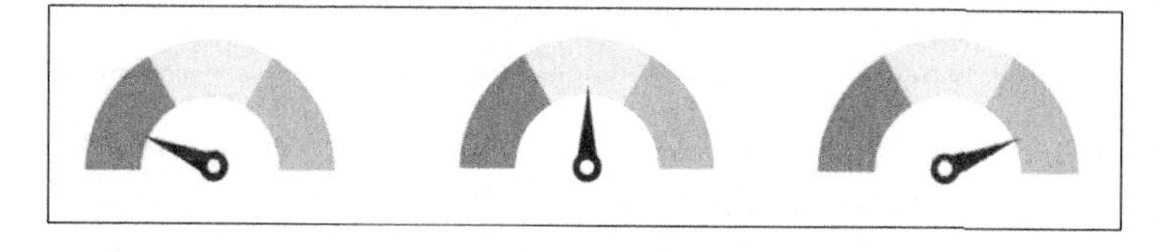

PROGRESS- METER REPORT

How well are you progressing as a couple?

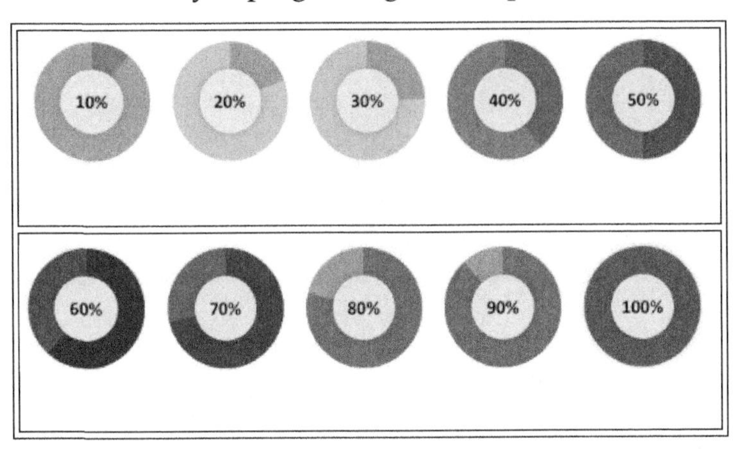

Summary Report:

- What areas do I need to work on?

- What areas will my spouse need to work on?

NOTES

CHECK OUT OUR MARRIAGE MINISTRY.

Website: https://www.positivevibrationglobal.com/couples-corner

COUPLES CORNER

Where God is best for you and your partner.

Building lasting and sustainable marriages through a variety of programs based on principles outlined in the scriptures. Marriage is the idea of God therefore we refer to him for the directives to create thriving unions.

Our Vision

To provide a safe space in which couples can thrive together physically and emotionally. To foster a community in which couples can be enriched through study, and practice of the principles outlined in scripture.

Our Mission

Our Mission is to become the leading provider of sound biblical, practical, and relatable knowledge and experiences for couples and singles alike equipping them to create successful marriages through the willing application of the principles set out in scripture.

Our Beliefs

- We believe God ordained marriages to be the base on which family should be developed.
- We believe marriage is the union of one man and one woman in a lifelong commitment that epitomizes Christ and His church.
- We believe husbands and wives are created equal by God and are uniquely designed in his image to represent his values in the earth.
- We believe that the Bible is the leading book that provide guidance to the couple.
- We believe in creating a success community to practice marriage effectively.

ADDITIONAL RESOURCE

21 Shades: A Practical Guide to Growing Intimacy in Marriage is designed to eradicate any presence of voided expressions of passion. This tool uniquely encompasses

doable stimulatory challenges which are proven tenets to releasing dopamine, serotonin, oxytocin and vasopressin, crucial hormones in the phenomenon of immersing in intimacy. The aforementioned does not only possess scientifically fancy sounds, but they are also going to reflect their competences to produce a high concentration of attraction, trust, empathy, effective communication, fidelity, rewards, and security, being strategically positioned in a vital section of the brain that influences the body's function, to include our affectionate relations.

BEFORE YOU SAY I DO: 21 Considerations to Ponder Before Constructing a Marriage.

"Don't sit around looking and fishing for every fish in the sea. When you see the one you love, plate it."- **Winston Peccoo** Marriage is a beautiful institution, and anyone desirous of taking the journey should be open to some of the key events and processes that will be important to the success of the union between them and the one they will plate.

Every piece of equipment comes with a manual that tells the user how to operate it according to the manufacturer's guidelines for maximum efficiency. No matter how experienced the user is, the instructions are usually clear enough that even a novice can fulfil the expectations with a significant level of mastery. Like all equipment, marriage requires support, understanding, and clarity. The idea of marriage is of God; therefore, the primary manual for ensuring a thriving marriage is the Bible. **Before you say I Do: 21 Considerations in Preparation for a Thriving Marriage,** however, is a tool intended to simplify and bring to light the principles guaranteeing a successful marriage, drawing from the author's own experiences alongside their psychological and educational expertise to bolster your awareness.

The writers intend to:

- Help singles discern and choose the right spouse for marriage.
- Prepare themselves to be the right person for marriage.
- Equip partners as a unit to become the right couple.

As you read, do so with a level of openness, bearing in mind that up to the lip the cup can slip. As you become conscious of marriage and its expectations you may choose to continue or discontinue your relationship to, I Do. Do so knowing it is better to wait long than to marry wrong. Do not become so imprisoned to the extent that you ignore the warnings signs of possible red flags with the hope of things becoming better. We have made it easy to track your progress as you go through this practical manual by adding knowledge gages that will help you to determine whether you will proceed, and if so, areas that could be improved with counselling, conversations and or alterations.

ABOUT THE AUTHORS

Nicholas and Danielle Robertson

THE ROBDONS

Nicholas Robertson hails from Mendez town, a rural farming community in the parish of Trelawny, a few miles out of Manchester. While Danielle Drown-Robertson was raised in the community of Sandside approximately 5km outside St Mary's capital, Port Maria. Nicholas is the first son and oldest child of Roger, a subsistence farmer, and Donna, a school vendor. Danielle is the daughter of Norman (minister, business owner) and Florence (minister, business owner, and teacher). Nicholas spent his formative years supporting his parents in farming and vending and soon became a farmer and vendor himself. He credits his parents for the managerial skills learned. On the other hand, Danielle is an avid money manager, and negotiator, skills she learned while aiding her parents in their business.

Nicholas attended Lowe River Basic School, Lowe River Primary School, and Knox College where he matriculated on to the University of West Indies and Christian Leaders College. Danielle commenced her education at J's Heart Ease Early Childhood, then went on to the Port Maria Primary school, Mary High School, Brown Town Community College, the University of West Indies, and the United Theological College of the West Indies. Nicholas' love for church and God dwindled during his teenage years but Danielle remained the avid "Preacher's Kid." Nicholas later became a Christian at fifteen and took on an active role in ministry at the Pentecostal Church of God the same organization to which Danielle served. The couple crossed paths at a General Convention in 2006 but never dated until 2010 during which time they were both first-year students in University and College. The couple got engaged in 2011 and tied the knot in 2013.

Amidst the differences in upbringing and family structures, the couple employed varying strategies to build a successful union. The union is blessed with two wonderful children, Danick in and Danice. Danielle and Nicholas actively serve in varying ministries: leadership, evangelism and discipleship, education and development, radio, and social media ministry. The couple has lived and work in Jamaica and the USA. They now live in England where

Nicholas is a Computer Science teacher at Fitzwimarc High School while Danielle is entrepreneur and philantraphist. Both Nicholas and Danielle were instrumental in starting the Positive Vibration 365 Plus Global Ministries, Impact Online Bible Institute, and BuildAMan Foundation Global which Nicholas serves as Director and Danielle Admin Director.

The couple is guided by the philosophy "bloom where you are planted." They host a daily devotional, a component of Positive Vibration 365+ Global on Reason with Robdon and Mr. and Mrs. Robdons Couples Corner on The Robdons where they share relationship tips and also stir discussions relating to the same.

Nicholas is the author of following books:

- Positive Vibration: Navigating through Difficult Times
- Positive Vibration: Biblical Keys for Faith Activation,
- Build A Man: A Mentorship Guide for Developing Men
- Critical Keys to Biblical Interpretation 1 and 2
- Critical Keys for Marketplace Evangelism
- Critical Keys for Financial Freedom

- Winning at Leading: A Critical Guide to Leadership and Administration.

Danielle has authored a powerful book for creating intimacy in marriage entitiled:

- 21 Shades: A Practical Guide to Growing Intimacy in Marriage

The couple together authors:

- Before You Say "I Do": 21 Considerations to Consider Before Constructing A Thriving Marriages
- After You Say "I Do" : 21 Considerations for Constructing Thriving Marriages

The couple hopes to ecosystem in which people can holistically develop and impact the world for good.

Printed in Great Britain
by Amazon